Dating
&
Waiting

Dating
&
Waiting

Looking for Love in
All the Right Places

WILLIAM P. RISK

kregel
PUBLICATIONS

Grand Rapids, MI 49501

Dating & Waiting: Looking for Love in All the Right Places

© 2000 by William P. Risk

Published by Kregel Publications, a division of Kregel, Inc., P.O. Box 2607, Grand Rapids, MI 49501. For more information about Kregel Publications, visit our web site: www.kregel.com

Unless otherwise indicated, Scripture quotations are taken from the NEW AMERICAN STANDARD BIBLE®, © The Lockman Foundation 1960, 1962, 1963, 1968, 1971, 1972, 1973, 1975, 1977, 1995. Used by permission. (www.Lockman.org)

Excerpt from THE JERUSALEM BIBLE, © Darton, Longman and Todd, Ltd., and Doubleday and Company, Inc. Reprinted by permission of the publisher.

Scripture quotations marked NIV are from the Holy Bible: New International Version®. © 1973, 1978, 1984 by International Bible Society. Used by permission of Zondervan Publishing House. All rights reserved.

Scripture quotations marked RSV are from the Revised Standard Version of the Bible, © 1946, 1952, 1971, 1973 by the Division of Christian Education of the National Council of the Churches of Christ in the United States of America.

Library of Congress Cataloging-in-Publication Data
Risk, William P.
    Dating and waiting: looking for love in all the right places / by William P. Risk
p. cm.
    1. Dating (Social customs). 2. Dating (Social customs)—Religious aspects—Christianity. I. Title.
HQ801.R565   2000   241'.6765—dc21   00-030974
                                                    CIP

ISBN 0-8254-3581-1

Printed in the United States of America

2 3 4 5 / 04 03 02 01

Contents

Preface

I started writing this book just before my thirtieth birthday. I was single then, wondering if I would ever be married. I began writing simply to try to organize and articulate what I thought I was learning about God through singleness and about singleness through Scripture. As time passed, I fell in love, got married, and became a father. Although no longer single, I continued rethinking and rewriting until, at length, what began as a series of essays written to untangle my own thoughts developed into a book manuscript. By the time I submitted the final manuscript to my publisher, it was just before my fortieth birthday. *Tempus fugit,* indeed!

Yet, even as my situation in life has changed, and the experiences of marriage and fatherhood have taught me new lessons about God, I find that I keep returning to the things I learned when I was single. There are two main reasons for that. The first is that when I look back on my life thus far, it was during those postcollege, premarriage years that I grew the most in my trust of Jesus. I think the same will be true for many readers of this book. Our single years are filled with great opportunity, with tremendous energy and enthusiasm, with challenges that seem as though they might crush us, and with uncertainty and self-doubt that frighten us. It is often during these times that we first encounter and face up to the great spiritual questions and struggles of life, when we take new ground in conquering spiritual Canaan. All these factors conspire to make this time of life stick in our memories.

The second reason is expressed well by the writer of Ecclesiastes: "What has been will be again, what has been done will be done again; there is nothing new under the sun" (1:9 NIV). The issues with which we struggle as single Christians are symptomatic of deeper ones that recur throughout our lifelong spiritual pilgrimage: "Do I really believe that God loves me?" "Can I really trust Him to know what I need and to provide it?" "Why isn't my life turning out the way I imagined it would?" "What will make my life fulfilling and satisfying?" Acquiring a biblical grid through which to view these issues when they first occur during our single years lays a solid foundation for dealing with them when they recur later in life in different contexts. I hope that the reader will find that the principles discussed in this book apply beyond the specific areas of singleness, dating, and marriage, even though that will be its focus.

I wish to take this opportunity to acknowledge some of the influences that have shaped the content of this book. I wandered into Peninsula Bible Church in Palo Alto, California, in late 1982, at the recommendation of a friend who liked John Fischer's music and knew that he had been based there. Little did I suspect what awaited me! The first time I heard Ray Stedman's expository preaching, my "heart burned within me," and I knew I had found a church home. And Ray was just one of several brilliant and gifted pastor-teachers in that place who taught me so much, so capably, over the years.

A few years after I began attending the church, some friends invited me to join a small-group Bible study they were starting for "postcollege, premarriage" men and women. My experiences in that group, which met regularly over a period of about seven years, first stimulated me to wonder how best to apply the teachings of the Bible to the issues of singleness, and profoundly shaped my thinking on that subject. It is probably not an exaggeration to say that were it not for that group, this book would never have come about.

Several friends from both categories—PBC pastor-teachers and fellow members of that singles group—have been kind enough to read and comment upon portions of this project at various stages of its evolution and to offer both encouragement and valuable suggestions for its improvement. Space does not permit me to name them individually (except for one, my wife, Kathy, who faithfully proofread the entire manuscript and offered many insightful observations), but I want each of them to know I am thankful.

Finally, Dennis Hillman, Janyre Tromp, Stephen Barclift, and Rachel Warren of Kregel Publications have been very kind, patient, and helpful in bringing this book to press, and I am grateful for their involvement.

chapter one

Taxonomy

The garden was cool and fragrant that morning. Adam awoke, refreshed from a sound night's sleep, just as the first hint of rose tinted the sky. He ate some of the sweet, succulent fruit of the garden and slaked his thirst with a palmful of cool, clear water from the stream. As he straightened up and stretched, he sensed a presence in the garden and heard the voice of the Eternal One.

"Adam? Where are you, Adam?"

"Here I am!" he replied.

God stepped into the clearing where Adam was waiting. "Adam," God said, "I have a job for you. You see all these animals that I have created? Birds in the air, fish in the stream, others all around? I want you to give them names."

"All of them?" Adam asked.

"Every last one," God replied.

So Adam set about doing the task that God had given him. He studied each animal and gave it a name that was descriptive of its unique characteristics. He marveled at the variety and complexity of the creatures that God had made and at His amazing creativity. He wondered at the diversity with which God had implemented similar functions. Ears, he noticed, came floppy or straight up, rounded or pointy, smooth or fuzzy, but all of them were designed for perceiving sound.

As Adam neared the end of his project, a growing realization stole upon him. Of all the animals that he had seen, none was like him! No other creature looked like him. No other creature thought or spoke as he did. None other was self-aware in quite the same way as he or quite so like the Eternal One. All of the creatures that he had named existed in two sexes—male and female—but so far, he had discovered no female counterpart to himself.

Perhaps it was with perplexity, perhaps with increasing despair and a growing realization of his aloneness, that Adam worked through the remaining animals. He no longer merely named them, but he also searched—for the one that was like him, the one that could be his mate and counterpart.

Separation and Preparation

Why did God give Adam the task of naming the animals? Why did not God, who created them, simply tell Adam what their names should be? It is true that God wanted to establish Adam's dominion over the rest of the animal kingdom, but there was another reason as well. God was taking Adam through a process—one that involved both separation and preparation.

It involved *separation,* in that God was showing Adam that he was unique and set apart from the other creatures that God had made. Adam alone among all of the creatures that he had seen enjoyed fellowship and spiritual communion with God. Adam must have come to realize that he occupied a special place in the created order, a special place in God's heart.

It involved *preparation* in that God was showing Adam his need for a mate and companion and was conditioning his heart to appreciate the gift that God had in store for him. God had no intention of squandering His final and most triumphant act of creation—woman—on an ungrateful and unappreciative man! So He showed Adam his need—not by telling him of it directly, but by placing Adam in a situation where he would discover it for himself. So it is with us as single Christians. From adolescence to matrimony, God takes us through a process of "naming the animals," our own odyssey of separation—learning our individual worth—and preparation—learning our need and thus being able to feel appreciation when God fulfills that need. Just as in Adam's case, God has both a *pedagogical* purpose and a *practical* purpose for the process. Ever the Great Pedagogue, He teaches us lessons through this odyssey that we could learn in no other way. He causes us to recognize our uniqueness and exquisite value to Him as individuals—before marriage. Thus, we may enter marriage secure in our own identities in Christ and complete in Him, and not expecting a spouse to be the source of that sense of identity and completeness.

Through the process He molds our hearts to appreciate the gift that He provides in a mate. He desires to cultivate in us a heart of thanksgiving—thanksgiving not solely in response to the specific gift of a mate but of general thanksgiving toward Him. Even if, in His sovereignty, He determines that a particular individual will remain single and never marry, the process can still shape godly character and develop skills and sensitivities in dealing with people. Those traits can have great impact as we go through life being "salt and light." By molding us and giving us a grateful heart, God takes us through part of the process of sanctification, cleansing us and setting us apart as useful vessels for His service. That is the ultimate result to which we should look with longing—marriage may or may not be a part of the plan (and we need the ability to submit to God's sovereignty in that regard). But we can rest assured that "he who began a good work in you will carry it on to completion until the day of Christ Jesus."[1]

In addition to a pedagogical purpose, God has a practical purpose for our single years. Adam was not given mere busywork to do; his task of animal-naming served a useful purpose apart from teaching him something. It brought order and perspective to his view of the animal kingdom, and the close familiarity with the animals that Adam gained by naming them enabled him to care for them more effectively. Seeing such an amazing variety of remarkable creatures must also have increased his sense of awe and wonder toward the One who had created them and drawn him more deeply into worship of God.

Single-Minded Servants

As unmarried men and women, we are called by God to purposeful ministries. He desires to show us that we are useful to Him as single individuals. He gives us jobs to do that can provide blessing to others and draw us into a more intimate acquaintance with Him. Not only is there much that God can teach us but also many ways that He can use us in the service of His kingdom.

We do a great disservice to God, to others, and to ourselves when we look upon our single years as a desolate wasteland best traversed quickly and, once traversed, quickly forgotten. We are all, whether single or married, called to be servants, and servants are not given the option of placing constraints on their service. They are not allowed to say, "I really don't feel like serving today," or more to the point, "I can't really serve God until He brings me a mate." If we truly believe the Scripture that tells us "you are not your own . . . you have been bought with a price,"[2] then dictating to God the conditions under which we will or will not serve Him is not an option.

A widespread misconception exists in the Christian church that the work of "ministry" is the sole province of those who are called to full-time, "formal" Christian service—those who have attended seminary, who are "on staff" with some Christian organization, or who possess the title *Pastor* or *Reverend.* This perception may be popular, but it is not biblical.[3] Every Christian is given spiritual gifts,[4] equipped with divine enablements to use for the proclamation of the gospel and the building up of the believing community. These gifts do not lie dormant while we are single, suddenly turning on in a burst of spiritual energy and enlightenment when the pastor says, "I now pronounce you man and wife"! They are there, waiting to be used, from the moment we become followers of Jesus. If we can muster the conviction to focus on Him and what He is calling us to do, rather than on ourselves and on our perceived needs (or wants), we make ourselves available to God for Him to use powerfully. Our single years, too, can provide unique opportunities for responding to God's call—opportunities that may not materialize in later life. The time, energy, and material resources that we can devote to ministry—and the spontaneity and intensity with which we can do so—are typically much greater during our single years than they are after we marry and start families.

The Dating Dilemma

In our time and culture, much of this process of "naming the animals" revolves around the peculiar social institution we call "dating." If an observer from the past—even as recently as the last century—were transported into the modern era, he or she would probably be astonished and appalled to observe how we find and choose our mates. For most of human history, matches were arranged by the families of the prospective bride and groom according to an orderly, prescribed procedure. Class differences and ethnic distinctions limited the pool of potential mates, and affection was a consideration secondary to the stability and socioeconomic elevation that was possible through an advantageous marriage. Our modern sensibilities are offended by the rigidity of these outmoded practices, as would be our time-traveler by what he or she would regard as the chaotic and tumultuous nature of our own practices.

The description of our dating rituals as "chaotic" and "tumultuous" is accurate, at least some of the time. We often find ourselves on an emotional roller coaster that undulates between confidence and uncertainty, elation and despair, pursuit and flight.

"Does he like me only as a friend or as something more?"

"Should I ask her out and risk being rejected or keep my feelings to myself?"

"What can I do to attract his attention without coming on too strongly?"

As dating singles, we make friends and lose them; we date and break up; we fall in love and fall out of love; we suffer rejection and reject others; we suffer broken hearts and break the hearts of others. These perils are common to anyone who dates, regardless of theological perspective. But as single men and women who are also followers of Jesus Christ, we are forced to grapple with additional issues.

"Is 'Christian dating' any different from the way the rest of the world dates? Should it be?"

"Is it acceptable for a Christian to date a non-Christian?"

"How can we be 'brothers and sisters in Christ' and deal with our romantic impulses?"

"How far can a relationship go physically before it becomes disobedient and dishonoring to God?"

As we should with every cultural institution, we ought to ask whether or not our modern dating practices are really consistent with the principles established by Scripture. Do our dating rituals conform to what the Bible says concerning the interaction of human beings with one another and with the furtherance of God's redemptive work? Considering this question requires a more thoughtful approach to both life and Scripture than most of us can sustain when our hormones are raging and we are caught up in what one friend calls "the swirling vortex of desire." But the reward for adopting such an approach is tremendous, and the consequences for failing to do so can be severe.

When single individuals and entire churches fail to appraise singleness and dating from a biblical perspective, the consequences can be harmful. More than most other ministries that are focused on a specific segment of the church body, singles groups often become places of turmoil, confusion, hurt, and distrust. Few singles groups of any size escape the unsavory reputation of being a "meet market," a refuge for both the perennially lonely and the socially predatory. What should be a wonderful opportunity for single Christians to exercise their spiritual gifts, to serve each another unselfishly, and to build up one another in love for Christ—unfettered by responsibilities of home and family— too often deteriorates into a "singles club" covered over with a thin veneer of Christian ministry. As a result, not only is the opportunity for spiritual growth and renewal often lost, but harm can be done. Men and women who are there for the pure fellowship in the body of Christ, for a chance to grow in their knowledge of the Lord, and for the opportunity to use their gifts without having their motives questioned or being "hit on," wind up discouraged and disillusioned, and they go elsewhere.

On an individual level, the intense emotions associated with dating, being single, and wanting to be married can cause us to lose our focus on God and what He is calling us to do. Our gaze can turn inward, and we can become absorbed with our own emotions, our own longings, our own dissatisfactions, our own unfulfilled desires. It is true that shifting our focus away from ourselves and toward God will always be a struggle. It is also true that we may find this struggle to be most intense in our single years. From adolescence to middle age, our emotions are most keen, our passions are most fervent, and our desires are most insistent. And simultaneously, our perspective is most limited, our spiritual armor is most untried, and our convictions are most easily overridden by our longings.

Hecataeus's Complaint

What is the solution to this state of affairs? How shall we deal with the issues of the single state and the frustrations that accompany it? Our search begins by scouring Scripture, by looking in God's own love letter to the human race. Cracking open our Bibles is probably not the first response that occurs to most of us for dealing with our unmarried state. When it comes to the sensitive issues of singleness, the Word of the Lord is the last place we might think to look. Instead, we might search the bestsellers written by self-help gurus and pop psychologists who proclaim that men are from one planet and women are from another. We might take the quizzes in popular magazines that purport to diagnose what is wrong with our love lives and then prescribe a cure. We might have soulful chats with trusted friends whom we consider to be wiser in the ways of love than we are. We might even take advantage of the latest information-gathering craze and "surf the web" to find sites where singles can chat electronically about the travails of love and life, locate resources to help them cope with the stresses of singleness, or even set up dates online.

Some of these sources of information may indeed have value. But by themselves, without the benchmark of Scripture against which to evaluate them, they can be deceptive, even dangerous. For those of us who proclaim ourselves followers and servants of Jesus Christ, Scripture should be the first place we turn when trying to understand what singleness, dating, and marriage are all about. We might not find all the answers, but we should emerge from our study with a better understanding of the mind of God on these issues.

We might have to dig for some of the answers—unfortunately, the canon of Scripture does not contain "The Letter of Paul to the Singles in Antioch" or "The Revelation to John about Dating." Our job would be easier if it did, but the search would be less rewarding. Benjamin Franklin observed with regard to liberty that "what we obtain too cheaply, we esteem too lightly," and maybe this aphorism applies equally well to the principles of living that we glean from the study of Scripture.

The ancient traveler and writer Hecataeus, writing about the Hebrew Scriptures (our Old Testament) some three centuries before the birth of Christ, bemoaned the fact that the world gave scant attention to those who honor the precepts contained therein:

> It is no wonder that authors, poets, and the common run of historians have failed to refer to these books and to the men who have lived and still live, in accordance with them: if they have been passed over in silence, that is not by chance, but because of the sacred matter that they contain.[5]

Some things have not changed much since Hecataeus's day. In its fallen state, human nature resists the counsel of Scripture. As Jeremiah proclaimed, "The heart is more deceitful than all else and is desperately sick; who can understand it?"[6] Like a dying man who refuses to take the only medicine that will save him because he finds it unpalatable, humanity generally has refused to heed what Scripture tells us about ourselves, even though that teaching is the only source of real truth about mankind and of our hope for happiness. The prophet Amos foresaw a time when there would be "not a famine for bread or a thirst for water, but rather for hearing the words of the Lord."[7] It often seems as though we are now living in such a time.

Swimming Elephants and Wading Lambs

But Scripture does speak accurately about the human heart and its longings. It truthfully diagnoses the disease that afflicts all humanity and prescribes the only effective cure. As Paul wrote to Timothy, "All Scripture is inspired by God and profitable for teaching, for reproof, for correction, for training in righteousness; so that the man of God may be adequate, equipped for every good work."[8]

Pope Gregory the Great is said to have remarked that "the Bible is a stream wherein the elephant may swim and the lamb may wade." I take that to mean two things: one, that Scripture offers insight into the issues of life, no matter how weighty or complex; two, that all who seek answers there—whether baby believers or ancient adherents—will find their efforts rewarded. The issues that concern unmarried Christians—their questions about singleness, dating, and marriage—are not outside the scope of biblical teaching.

Scripture is a mirror[9] into which—if we muster sufficient courage and honesty—we can gaze. It reveales us as we truly are, in all the glory—albeit dimmed—with which we were created, and in all the shabby disarray of our fallen state. Many of us turn away from this reflection, unable or unwilling to face what we see. But it's better to know that there is a speck of spinach on your tooth or that your hair is sticking up strangely, and be able to correct the defect, than to plunge on through life in blind ignorance of the fact! And, if I understand James rightly, those who have the courage and honesty to gaze into that mirror and not turn away are transformed by their obedience and by God's grace from this present state of disarray to one of ultimate splendor.

Scripture is also a source of illumination: "Your word is a lamp to my feet and a light to my path."[10] It makes clearly visible that which is otherwise only dimly perceived. This enlightenment has a purpose—not merely to make us aware of our situation but to enable us to navigate through it. We cannot move without difficulty and danger in the absence of light (try walking around a wilderness campsite on a moonless night with no flashlight!); thus, we are content to sit immobile in the dark where it is comfortable, familiar, and safe. The presence of light invites the movement that darkness inhibits. Scripture does not merely illuminate; it also facilitates the spiritual progress that its illumination both suggests and enables.

And so, in the pages that follow, we will begin the process of discovering what Scripture reveals about singleness and dating. As we turn the pages of the Word together and dig into its rich truths about who we are, who God is, and what He requires of us, we need to keep open minds. We must be prepared not only to embrace the encouragement of Scripture, but also to consider honestly the conviction that it produces in our hearts—to rejoice when we find that we are living in accord with the Word but to repent when we find that we are not.

In the end—in the eternal scheme of things—it probably matters little whom we marry or whether we marry at all. Although God cares about these things (at least as much as we do), what matters even more to Him is that we enter into a relationship with Him, and that we grow in that relationship, ever more closely resembling His Son. He accomplishes that purpose by means that are different for each of us; for some people this purpose will involve marriage, for others it will not. But regardless, we can rest assured that as we "name the animals," God will work in us to teach us, to refine us, and to conform us to the likeness of His Son— and that in itself is more than ample reward for the labor.

Consider This

1. How far along are you in the process of "naming the animals"? Near the beginning? Near the end? Why do you think so?
2. In what ways does your church address the needs of its single people? In what ways does it fail?
3. What are the three biggest issues, questions, or concerns that you as a single person face?

chapter two

Paradigm Lost /
Paradigm Regained

I would not ask Thee why
My path should be
Through strange and stony ways—
Thou leadest me!
I would not ask Thee how
Loss worketh gain,
Knowing that some day soon—
All shall be plain.
My heart would never doubt
Thy love and care,
However heavy seems
The cross I bear,
Nor would I, Father, ask
My lot to choose,
Lest seeking selfish ease
Thy best I lose.

—Grace E. Troy

According to *Webster's Third International Dictionary* (un-abridged), a paradigm (PAIR-a-dime) is a pattern or model. The word is derived from the Greek, meaning "setting side-by-side."

For a long time, this word remained pretty much the

exclusive possession of linguists, who used it to describe a pattern for conjugating verbs, declining nouns, and the like. However, in the past decade or two, it has become trendy to talk of paradigms as patterns of thinking or behaving, and the word has become a familiar part of our everyday vocabulary. Phrases such as "shifting your paradigm" are tossed about to describe solving problems in new and imaginative ways. Technical folk are encouraged to overcome mental blocks when solving engineering and scientific problems by casting off old paradigms and adopting new ones, by getting beyond their preconceptions and unstated suppositions. It has been argued, in fact, that scientific revolutions occur when the entrenched paradigms governing the thinking of scientists are overthrown and replaced by new ones.[1]

For us Christians, the process of coming to faith is really the ultimate change in paradigm. Isn't that the essence of what Paul means when he says, "Do not be conformed to this world, but be transformed by the renewing of your mind"?[2] How we think, how we act, how we feel—everything about us—is gradually rewritten to conform to God's pattern. God is the ultimate paradigm shifter—He is the Author, Initiator, and Executor of the changes.

Jesus is the ultimate exemplar of God's paradigm; His earthly life as recorded in the Gospels provides an example of what God's paradigm looks like when it is lived out to the fullest in humanity. Throughout Scripture, we catch glimpses of God at work in the lives of other men and women, and their stories provide us with pictures of what the work-in-progress looks like. We have other examples in our living contemporaries. As we look at our brothers and sisters in Christ, we see them in the process of transformation, in the middle of having their own paradigms overthrown in favor of God's paradigm.

In the area of romantic relationships, God often does a

lot of paradigm shifting. Most of us approach adulthood with a nonbiblical view of relationships. Not only do we often have excess baggage as a result of growing up in a fallen world but we inherit bad paradigms for relationships from others, even Christians. Well-meaning friends tell us about how they met their spouses and we think, "Maybe it will happen the same way for me." Consider the following examples:

- A couple were oblivious to each other until they happened to be riding in the same car to a church retreat and were forced to spend several additional hours in each other's company after the car broke down.
- A woman's first impression of the man she would eventually marry was that he was a total jerk—until something happened to make her see him differently.
- A man decided that God did not intend for him to get married. He "renounced women" and focused on serving the Lord. Then one day a particular woman came into his life and completely overthrew his paradigm.

It is fascinating to hear stories of how people met their mates, and it is easy to adopt these examples as paradigms by which we evaluate our own potential relationships. The next time we carpool to a church retreat, we find ourselves saying, "Maybe the car will break down and love will blossom as I get to know someone familiar in a new light." We meet someone we think is rather obnoxious, but in the back of our minds we think, "But maybe he'll turn out to be the one after all." We resolve to set our hearts anew on doing what God puts before us, but somewhere deep inside we think, "Maybe He'll bring me a wife the way He did for that other fellow."

"As Someday It May Happen That a Victim Must Be Found, I've Got a Little List, I've Got a Little List. . . ."[3]

We sometimes express paradigms as a list of attributes that our spouse must have. When we meet someone who satisfies enough of the criteria, we think of that person as a prime candidate. The comic strip "Bliss" tells the story of a young married couple named Steven and Dana. In one episode, as they are dancing, we overhear the following exchange:

DANA: "I can't believe I married someone who can't dance."

STEVEN: "I'm sorry."

DANA: "Dancing was so high on my list of husband must-haves."

STEVEN: "Instead you got a collection of husband characteristics you never dreamed you'd have access to."

DANA: "Double-jointed thumbs, encyclopedic knowledge of Gilbert and Sullivan . . ."

STEVEN: "Ability to imitate a pump bottle . . ." (said as he holds both arms over his head, fingers crooked in imitation of the pump-action of a spray bottle).[4]

We may think of our lists as profound reflections of our innermost desires. Viewed objectively, however, some of the items on our lists often seem silly. A woman in a college Bible study that I once attended insisted that she could marry only a U.S. senator or a man clearly on the path to becoming one. I think I remember Elisabeth Elliot saying in one of her talks that the only item on her list that Jim Elliot did not possess was an operatic voice. The "Bliss" strip quoted above caught my eye because an appreciation of Gilbert and Sullivan was once one of the items on *my* list.

While our lists contain things that we want a potential

spouse to have, they also contain characteristics that automatically cause us to reject someone. Some college-age folk will not "date outside their fellowship group"—if they are in InterVarsity, they would not even consider dating someone from Navigators or Campus Crusade. Others would not consider someone who goes to "that church." Some would not consider a person who hadn't gone to seminary or wasn't considering a full-time career in ministry. Everyone has their own criteria: "I could never marry someone who isn't as athletic as I am," "I could never marry someone who doesn't like music as much as I do," "I could never marry someone who would drive that kind of car," and so on.

God often delights in showing us how ridiculous our criteria are. One woman I know thought that she could never marry a man who was shorter than she was, and another woman was horrified at the idea of marrying a man even slightly younger than she was. Guess what happened to both of them? C. S. Lewis, the sedate, middle-aged Oxford don, wound up married to a brash, opinionated, Jewish, excommunist, American divorcee nearly twenty years his junior. Lewis, the confirmed bachelor, was embarrassed by having fallen in love, and most of his friends disliked the woman. But he later reckoned the few years that they were married as among the happiest of his life.[5]

In addition to criteria that are silly, most of us have more meaningful benchmarks on our lists: a love for God, a passion for serving Him, a willingness to live sacrificially, a respect for the authority of the Bible, and solid moral values, to name a few. Those criteria reflect our recognition that a godly marriage must be based on certain crucial shared values and on a shared perspective of life. But I wonder if—when our lists expand beyond those foundational elements to include such things as senatorial potential, operatic vocal cords, and a passion for Gilbert and Sullivan—we are really becoming more concerned with reducing the risk and difficulty of relationship-building than we are with finding someone who will complement and challenge us in a dynamic and growing relationship. Are we looking for artificial "signs" to help us determine which person is "the one"? Are we avoiding the hard, time-consuming, and sometimes painful work of getting to know someone well enough as a brother or sister in Christ to evaluate the potential for something deeper?

"There Must Be Fifteen Ways to Meet Your Lover. . . ."[6]

Amid the information circulating on the Internet is a list of the "Top Fifteen Biblical Ways to Acquire a Wife." I do not know the original author, else I would willingly give that person due credit. The list is as follows:

1. Find an attractive prisoner of war, bring her home, shave her head, trim her nails, and give her new clothes. Then she's yours (Israelites, Deut. 21:11–13).
2. Find a prostitute and marry her (Hosea, Hos. 1:1–3).
3. Find a man with seven daughters and impress him by watering his flock (Moses, Exod. 2:16–21).
4. Purchase a piece of property and get a woman as part of the deal (Boaz, Ruth 4:5–10).
5. Go to a party and hide. When the women come out to dance, grab one and carry her off to be your wife (Benjamites, Judg. 21:19–25).
6. Have God create a wife for you while you sleep. Note: this will cost you a rib (Adam, Gen. 2:19–24).
7. Agree to work seven years in exchange for a woman's hand in marriage. Get tricked into marrying the wrong woman. Then work another seven years for the woman you wanted to marry in the first place. That's right. Fourteen years of toil for a woman (Jacob, Gen. 29:15–30).

8. Cut off two hundred foreskins of your future father-in-law's enemies and get his daughter for a wife (David, 1 Sam. 18:27).

9. Even if no one is out there, just wander around a bit and you'll definitely find someone; it's all relative of course (Cain, Gen. 4:16–17).

10. Become the emperor of a huge nation and hold a beauty contest (Xerxes, or Ahasuersus, Esther 2:3–4).

11. When you see someone you like, go home and tell your parents, "I have seen a . . . woman; now get her for me." If your parents question your decision, simply say, "Get her for me. She's the one for me" (Samson, Judg. 14:1–3).

12. Kill any husband and take his wife, but be prepared to lose four sons (David, 2 Sam. 11–12:7).

13. Wait for your brother to die, then take his widow. It's not just a good idea; it's the law (Onan and Boaz, prescribed in Deuteronomy and Leviticus, example in Ruth).

14. Don't be so picky. Make up for quality with quantity (Solomon, 1 Kings 11:1–3).

15. A wife? NOT! (Paul, 1 Cor. 7:32–35).

The anonymous author of this list has done us a favor. He gives us a starting point for examining how characters in Scripture "met" their mates. Because this list is intended to be humorous, we might forgive its flippant presentation and recognize that it only scratches the surface of something that is much, much deeper.

Take item 2, for example. Its glib gloss on the story of Hosea and Gomer doesn't begin to do justice to that heart-rending tale. No matter how silly our lists may get, no man puts "harlot" among the characteristics he seeks in a bride. Yet God instructed Hosea to marry just such a woman—one whom he knew would become unfaithful to him and leave him and their children for another man, and then another, and then another. Eventually, cast off by her lovers and left destitute and broken by her harlotry, she was sold as a slave on the auction block. Hosea bought her back and restored her to a position of honor and intimacy by his side. Is there a more poignant picture of what it means to be rescued from our spiritual harlotry, bought out of slavery that we might stand as the bride of Christ, loved and given an undeserved place of honor?

Or take items 4 and 13, which relate to the story of Ruth and Boaz. The story opens with a couple from Bethlehem, Elimelech and Naomi, and their two sons, Mahlon and Chilion. They left their hometown during a time of famine and lived for a while as resident aliens in the land of Moab. During their long sojourn in Moab, Elimelech died. The sons grew up and married Moabite women, but both sons died before they could produce children. Thus, there was no male heir to perpetuate the line of Elimelech, a grievous circumstance in ancient Israel. According to Israelite law, when a man died before producing a son, his brother was supposed to marry his widow and raise up sons in his name. This practice is known as "the law of the levir" or "levirate marriage" (from the Latin word for "brother-in-law"[7]), and it is to this that item 13 refers.

But Naomi was well beyond childbearing years, and there was no hope that she could produce another son to fulfill the levirate duties with her daughters-in-law, Ruth and Orpah. Naomi decided to return to her native Bethlehem, and implored Ruth and Orpah to stay in Moab and return to their mothers so that they might find new husbands among the Moabites. Eventually, Orpah remained, but Ruth was adamant that she would accompany her mother-in-law back to Bethlehem, even though as a Moabite she would be viewed there as an unwelcome outsider. In declaring this intention, she uttered the famous verse that often finds its way into Christian wedding ceremonies, though it was spoken in a much different context:

> "Do not urge me to leave you or turn back from following you; for where you go, I will go, and where you lodge, I will lodge. Your people shall be my people, and your God, my God. Where you die, I will die, and there I will be buried. Thus may the LORD do to me, and worse, if anything but death parts you and me."[8]

After arriving in Bethlehem, Ruth gleaned grain from the periphery of a field, which, according to Israelite law, was to be left unharvested for the support of the needy. Unbeknownst to Ruth the field was owned by Boaz, a man of wealth and stature, who was a relative of Naomi's late husband. Boaz took an interest in Ruth and accorded her special favor in her gleaning, because, as he told her,

> "All that you have done for your mother-in-law after the death of your husband has been fully reported to me, and how you left your father and your mother and the land of your birth, and came to a people that you did not previously know. May the LORD reward your work, and your wages be full from the LORD, the God of Israel, under whose wings you have come to seek refuge."[9]

When Naomi learned that Ruth had been gleaning in the fields of Boaz, she recognized his name as that of a close relative. In fact, she described him as a *gōʾēl*. In ancient Israel a *gōʾēl* was a kinsman who could act as a redeemer, buying back property sold by a near relative or redeeming a family member who had sold himself or herself into slavery. A *gōʾēl* could also exact a "blood debt" for the murder of a family member by killing the murderer or one of his kin, or act as a trustee to collect payment associated with the wrongdoing committed against a deceased clan member. Boaz's position, then, was one of great responsibility and protection. When Naomi realized that a *gōʾēl* was at hand, she encouraged Ruth to present herself before him and ask his aid for Ruth and Naomi. Naomi likely had in mind the possibility that Boaz might consider marriage to Ruth as part of his duties as a *gōʾēl*.

Following Naomi's suggestion, Ruth bathed, perfumed herself, dressed in her finest frock, and went down to the threshing floor, where Boaz would be spending the night guarding the winnowed barley. Naomi instructed Ruth to wait patiently for the right moment to approach Boaz. She was to wait until he had fallen asleep, then she was to uncover his feet so that he would awaken when the night air grew cool and made him uncomfortable. She was to lie down at his feet, in the position of a suppliant, until he awoke.

When Boaz awoke, Ruth asked him to "spread your covering over your maid, for you are a close relative."[10] In Ruth's request for this covering, Hebrew scholars note a word play that alludes to Boaz's earlier prayer that God "spread his wing" protectively over Ruth. The allusion suggests that Boaz himself is about to become the instrument by which his own petition for God's protection of Ruth is answered and by which her past kindness to Naomi is paid in full.[11]

Boaz agreed to Ruth's request because, he said, "all my people in the city know that you are a woman of excellence."[12] He pointed out, however, a potential obstacle to their union—the existence of an even closer kinsman whose claim superseded his own. Boaz approached the other kinsman the next day and asked if he was willing to act as *gōʾēl* and redeem Elimelech's property (here we finally return to item 4). The closer kinsman said yes, but then Boaz revealed that acting as *gōʾēl* would also require acting as levir to Ruth the Moabitess and raising up an heir in Elimelech's name. The other kinsman demured, since the property he redeemed would go to Ruth's heir rather than to his own. Boaz then steped in as *gōʾēl*, claiming the property and Ruth. They were married, and eventually Ruth had a son, an heir for Elimelech, whom they named Obed. Obed became the grandfather of David, king of Israel.

Many aspects of this story are unique to the culture of the ancient Israelites. Thus we should have some reluctance in trying to make it a paradigm for establishing a match today. In Silicon Valley, where I live, many start-up companies have the reputation of being places were people work nonstop, catching only a few scant hours of sleep curled up under the desks in their cubicles. One could imagine a young woman seeking out a prospective husband in such an environment. She might creep into his cubicle late at night after he had fallen asleep, remove the jacket under which he was sleeping (or turn up the air conditioning) so that he would awaken, and lie at his feet until he did.

I would not encourage such behavior, but we can glean a few principles from the story of Ruth that are of value in suggesting how modern relationships should proceed. The honor with which Boaz treated Ruth and his concern for her reputation are noteworthy, particularly since she was a foreigner. Even before he met her, Boaz had heard of the sacrificial love that she extended to Naomi. On the basis of this knowledge Boaz was disposed to act favorably toward Ruth in spite of her Moabite ancestry, and thus her possible rejection by Israelite society. He was ready to go beyond what might legally be required of a *gōʾēl*, offering marriage on the basis of her excellent reputation. On the night that she approached him on the threshing floor, he instructed her to remain with him where it was safe, so that she would come to no harm in going home in the middle of the night. The next morning, Boaz was concerned that Ruth's departure from the threshing floor not be seen, thereby causing their meeting to be misconstrued as a clandestine sexual liaison. Thus, we are told in Ruth 3:14 that they "rose before one could recognize another" and that Boaz's concern was that "it not be known that the woman came to the threshing floor." Throughout, he acted as a man of honor and integrity, never pushing his claim or attempting to advance his own interests, but acting out of love for Ruth and Naomi.

Note, too, that even though Ruth's action, taken at Naomi's behest, might be seen as somewhat brash, there is a certain delicacy about it. Ruth did not charge up to Boaz and ask that he marry her. She waited patiently for an opportune moment, then indicated her interest in a way that was clear but consistent with the customs of her adopted country. She then left the decision and responsibility up to Boaz.

One final point of which to take note. We are not told whether Boaz was looking for a wife or what might have been included on his list of characteristics for the ideal wife. Chances are, however, his list did not contain such things as "from a foreign land, possibly Moab," "recently widowed," or "caring for a dependent mother-in-law." Yet that is precisely the kind of bride that God brought to Boaz, and through that union came David, and from David, Jesus. Ruth might not have been looking for an older man, but that is who God brought to her. And it seems to have been Boaz's kindness, his generous nature, his sacrificial love that attracted her, not his appearance or his station.

Number 16?

The witty author of the preceding "Top Fifteen Biblical Ways to Acquire a Wife" missed one: Instruct your most trusted servant to travel to your homeland and pick out a wife for your son. But that is just what Abraham did when he sought a wife for his son Isaac, as we read in Genesis 24:

Now Abraham was old, advanced in age; and the LORD had blessed Abraham in every way. Abraham said to his servant, the oldest of his household, who had charge of all that he owned. "Please place your hand under my thigh, and I will make you swear by the LORD, the God of heaven and the God of earth, that you shall not take a wife for my son from the daughters of the Canaanites, among whom I live, but you will go to my country and to my relatives, and take a wife for my son Isaac." The servant said to him, "Suppose the woman is not willing to follow me to this land; should I take your son back to the land from where you came?" Then Abraham said to him, "Beware that you do not take my son back there! The LORD, the God of heaven, who took me from my father's house and from the land of my birth, and who spoke to me and who swore to me, saying, 'To your descendants I will give this land,' He will send His angel before you, and you will take a wife for my son from there. But if the woman is not willing to follow you, then you will be free from this my oath; only do not take my son back there." So the servant placed his hand under the thigh of Abraham his master, and swore to him concerning this matter.[13]

Now I doubt that even the most literal interpreter of the Bible would advocate this story as a paradigm today for finding a wife (especially for himself). In our time and culture, fathers do not find wives for their sons in this way. So while the details of the story do not give us a recipe for finding a spouse, some of its principles are worthy of consideration.

Abraham had grown old, yet his faith had grown deeper. God had called him out of Ur into the land of the Canaanites to make him the father of a great nation through whom all the nations of the earth would be blessed.[14] The perpetuation of this promise is evidently in his mind as he summons his most senior and trusted servant and commissions him to find a wife for Isaac, the heir to God's promise.

Notice first that Abraham seeks a wife for Isaac "not . . . from the daughters of the Canaanites" but from "my father's house." The Canaanites were notorious for their debauchery and licentiousness. So while plenty of women were available locally, Abraham sends his servant some five hundred miles back to Mesopotamia to find a wife for Isaac. Abraham is quite adamant that his son's wife not be a woman from among the Canaanites, who did not honor his God. He insists that Isaac's bride be a person who is "spiritually compatible" with him.

Abraham refuses to compromise on this point. The servant anticipates the possibility that once he finds a suitable woman, she might not be thrilled with the idea of moving to a far-off land to marry a man whom she has never met. He suggests taking Isaac with him should that contingency arise. Abraham strictly forbids it! So serious is he about this entire matter that he makes the servant take an oath through the rather odd-seeming act of placing a hand under Abraham's "thigh" or "loins." It is from the loins that procreation proceeds. Thus, the manner of the oath probably indicated that its subject was so serious that violation of it was to be avenged not only by Abraham but also by his descendants.

Abraham's concern for the spiritual compatibility of Isaac's wife should give us food for thought. Do we take spiritual compatibility as seriously when looking for our own mates as Abraham did when looking for Isaac's mate? To what extent are we willing to protect ourselves from becoming entangled in relationships with persons who do not share our theological perspectives and convictions?

Another point worth noting is that Abraham relies not on his own discernment, nor on that of his trusted servant, nor even on Isaac's to find the right wife. He places the matter entirely before God: "The LORD, the God of heaven, who took me from my father's house and from the land of my birth, and who spoke to me and who swore to me, saying, 'To your descendants I will give this land,' He will send His angel before you, and you will take a wife for my son from there."[15] Abraham's statement emphasizes the characteristics of God that cause Abraham to rely on His judgment:

- His authority and sovereignty: ". . . who took me from my father's house and from the land of my birth"
- His personal communication: ". . . who spoke to me"
- His personal, covenantal obligation: ". . . who swore to me"

He trusts God as one whose authority he knows, who has spoken to him in the past, and who has demonstrated that He can be trusted to keep His promises.

Do we trust God enough to rely on His discernment and direction—rather than on our own discernment or that of our friends—as we seek a mate? Is our own relationship with Him so well-developed, so intimate, so seasoned that we can trust in His authority and sovereignty, in His communication with us, and in His promise-keeping character to find the right mates for us?

Abraham further tells his servant that "He will send His angel before you" as he seeks a wife for Isaac. Can we likewise trust in God's prelusive work as we seek our mates? Can we take as a general principle that when we find the persons whom we are to marry, God will have gone before us and prepared the way? That He will have readied our hearts for marriage at that time and with those persons?

That He will have similarly prepared the hearts of the other persons?

Abraham's faithful servant set out for the city of Nahor in Mesopotamia. He took with him ten camels and a variety of gifts for the prospective bride. Upon arriving,

> [H]e made the camels kneel down outside the city by the well of water at evening time, the time when women go out to draw water. He said, "O LORD, the God of my master Abraham, please grant me success today, and show lovingkindness to my master Abraham. Behold, I am standing by the spring, and the daughters of the men of the city are coming out to draw water; now may it be that the girl to whom I say, 'Please let down your jar so that I may drink,' and who answers, 'Drink, and I will water your camels also'—may she be the one whom You have appointed for Your servant Isaac; and by this I will know that You have shown lovingkindness to my master."[16]

Abraham's servant arrives in Nahor faced with a daunting task. Even granting that his choice of a bride for Isaac comes not from his own wisdom but from recognizing the one whom God has already chosen, how is he to do that? He does something logical—goes to a place where he is likely to find a large number of young women. He goes to a city well where, in the normal rhythm of daily life in that culture, he would expect to find the daughters of the families living nearby coming to draw water in the evening.

From the servant's action, some people might conclude that to find a mate, one should go to where the odds of doing so are highest. One should become involved with church singles groups, or go on cruises catering to single Christians, or enroll in a Christian dating service. Perhaps this is good, practical advice. But perhaps a few other factors are worth considering. First, we do not see Isaac himself on the prowl for a date. Rather, someone else acts on his behalf—someone older, wiser, and more objective. Second, the women showing up at the well were not there to find husbands. They were simply performing the tasks required as part of everyday life. So to be true to the story, single Christians would focus on the business of living and of serving others and let those who are older and wiser contemplate possible matches. As has been already acknowledged, this method would not be popular today. But making the argument provides counterbalance to those who might use these verses to sanction church singles groups that are essentially Christian pick-up spots or to justify cruising from one Bible study to another in search of a new dating pool.

Having arrived at a likely place to find a bride for Isaac, what does the servant do next? He does not survey the assembled cast to find the prettiest face or begin chatting them up to see who might make a good match. No, the first thing he does is pray. And the focal point of his prayer is the "lovingkindness" that God has consistently displayed toward Abraham. This is the same "loyal-love"—which in Hebrew is called *chesed*—that is the focal point of the story of Ruth and Boaz and the story of Hosea and Gomer.

The servant's prayer tells us something. Given our earlier discussion of the silly signs for which we look to help us identify a potential mate, we might either scoff at the servant's request that God, through a specific action, make clear the chosen woman, or we could use his request to justify our petition for the same. However, what strikes me in this account is the sign for which the servant asked—not one that was fribbling or frivolous, but one that indicated that the woman had the character for which Abraham hoped. The sign that the servant requested was a sign of servanthood.

He was looking for someone who would respond with hospitality to a weary, well-traveled stranger, who would graciously volunteer to do the hard work of watering ten tired, thirsty camels. It is said that a thirsty camel can drink up to twenty-one gallons of water in only ten minutes. Even if these camels drank only one-fourth that much, Rebekah would have had to haul fifty gallons of water—a total weight of four hundred pounds taking perhaps ten or twenty trips to the well. She was a servant, indeed!

Before he had finished speaking, behold, Rebekah who was born to Bethuel the son of Milcah, the wife of Abraham's brother Nahor, came out with her jar on her shoulder. The girl was very beautiful, a virgin, and no man had had relations with her; and she went down to the spring and filled her jar and came up. Then the servant ran to meet her, and said, "Please let me drink a little water from your jar." She said, "Drink, my lord"; and she quickly lowered her jar to her hand, and gave him a drink. Now when she had finished giving him a drink, she said, "I will draw also for your camels until they have finished drinking." So she quickly emptied her jar into the trough, and ran back to the well to draw, and she drew for all his camels. Meanwhile, the man was gazing at her in silence, to know whether the LORD had made his journey successful or not. When the camels had finished drinking, the man took a gold ring weighing a half-shekel and two bracelets for her wrists weighing ten shekels in gold, and said, "Whose daughter are you? Please tell me, is there room for us to lodge in your father's house?" She said to him, "I am the daughter of Bethuel, the son of Milcah, whom she bore to Nahor." Again she said to him, "We have plenty of both straw and feed, and room to lodge in." Then the man bowed low and worshipped the Lord. He said, "Blessed be the Lord, the God of my master Abraham, who has not forsaken His loving-kindness and His truth toward my master; as for me, the Lord has guided me in the way to the house of my master's brothers."[17]

The servant had barely finished his prayer for a sign before God answered it. It almost seems as if God is showing an eagerness, an impatience to demonstrate His lovingkindness to Abraham! Rebekah provides the precise indication that the servant had requested: in response to the servant's request for a drink, she offers to water his camels as well. Not only was she a servant but also she was beautiful and sexually pure. Does God answer prayer abundantly or what?

There is one sentence in the preceding paragraph that seems particularly telling. It says that even after Rebekah had fulfilled the sign that the servant requested, he did not immediately reveal his true purpose but "was gazing at her in silence, to know whether the Lord had made his journey successful or not." It must have taken her some time to water ten thirsty camels, giving the servant a chance to her observe her demeanor, to ensure that his first impression was a valid one, to verify that her character was consistent with her words. Are we as careful as he in evaluating those with whom we become romantically entangled? If persons match up well with our "little lists," do we jump right in or do we take the extra step of observing them for a time to become better acquainted with the character of those persons?

As we envision what it might be like one day to meet our mates and as we imagine what those persons will be like, doesn't it behoove us to take a step back and ask whether or not our hopes and expectations are founded on qualities of importance and significance? If we are more concerned about a future mate's golf score or knowledge of *Star Trek* trivia than the quality of his or her character or commitment to live a life devoted to Jesus, shouldn't that give us pause? Of course, if those deeper aspects are present, sharing common interests and enthusiasms is wonderful—it helps cement friendships that we hope will last a lifetime. But such common interests by themselves are not strong enough to hold a marriage together.

When we cling too tenaciously to particular expectations of what a future spouse will be like or how we will meet that person, we artificially limit our anticipation of how God will work, and we fail to do justice to both His creativity and His desire to bless and delight us. Just as happens in the realm of science, letting go of our old relationship paradigms can usher in a revolution, accompanied by exciting discoveries, new realizations, and a refreshed sense of wonder. Are we willing to let go of our old, cherished preconceptions—many of them laid down in childhood—and accept the likelihood that the best mates for us might not be U.S. senators, operatic singers, or compendia of Gilbert and Sullivan trivia or persons who are exceptionally good-looking or well-dressed? When we let go of our preconceptions, are we willing to be surprised and amazed by what God will bring us?

Consider This

1. Do you have a list of attributes for a future mate? How do you think each of those attributes will contribute to the strength of your marriage?
2. Do you have a preconceived expectation about how you will meet your spouse? On what is it based?
3. Go back to the list of "Top Fifteen Biblical Ways to Acquire

a Wife." Look at the Scripture references accompanying them, and see if you can extract from them any additional insights into what we should look for in a mate and how.

chapter three

Satisfiction

Why do you spend money for what is not bread, And your wages for what does not satisfy? (Isaiah 55:2)

There was a song that played over and over again on the radio when I was a child, and I've never quite gotten it out of my mind. It dealt with a man who longed for a certain woman but couldn't have her because she was involved with someone else. Eventually, circumstances changed, and she became his—but the results weren't exactly what he had in mind. The song went like this:

> I'd like to be in Charlie's shoes, that's what I always said,
> 'Cause he had you, and everything tied with a golden thread.
> Then Charlie left and went away, and when I got the news,
> It wasn't long 'til I was walkin' round in Charlie's shoes.

> Now I'm wearing out the shoes that Charlie wore,
> Walkin' back and forth across the floor.

The troubles that drove him away, I've got for
company—
These nights in Charlie's shoes are killin' me.

The greener grass that turned my head so swiftly
did turn brown,
'Cause every little dream I build she's always
tearin' down.
I never knew old Charlie's shoes could have so
many tacks
Of disappointing sorrows and I wish he had 'em
back.

'Cause I'm wearing out the shoes that Charlie
wore,
Walkin' back and forth across the floor.
The troubles that drove him away, I've got for
company.
These nights in Charlie's shoes are killin' me.[1]

We are sometimes afflicted with a remarkable shortsight-edness when it comes to pursuing what we want. We think that there is a magic key to contentment—something that, once possessed, will unlock the happiness and satisfaction that we deserve. This notion is hard to shake. But often when we get what we want, we find that the object of our obsession fails to satisfy, or we find that it has a "down side" on which we never reckoned. "Walkin' in Charlie's shoes"—living his lifestyle, having his woman—looked good to the singer, until he actually got them. Then he discovered that having was less satisfying than wanting.

Sometimes we get what we want and find that it is actually as satisfying as we had hoped—but only for a while. Eventually the novelty wears off, and we find ourselves saying, "Ah, I thought it was this I wanted, but now I see it is really that instead." Like those Russian matroyshka dolls that nest one inside the other, there is always one more want inside the current one. When the current want is satisfied, another want takes its place.

While I was vacationing with some friends and their children, we stopped at a souvenir shop. The kids discovered T-shirts that they just had to have. If they could not have these T-shirts their childhoods would be irrevocably damaged—they would become dropouts, drug addicts, and serial killers—or so they led Mom to believe. They pleaded, eyes welling with tears, lower lips quivering, for these T-shirts, which had suddenly become the *sine qua non* of their existence.

"Just this one, Mom—please, just this one!" they cried. "I won't ask for anything else if I can have just this one!"

Funny thing, though—after Mom gave in and bought those T-shirts, the scenario was repeated at the next store. Now this store had the one essential T-shirt, the one without which life itself would be banal and devoid of meaning. And so on and so on.

I observed this melodrama with amusement, remembering that I had used much the same tactics when I was a child. However, my amusement quickly turned to sober contemplation when I realized that I still act out this same fiction as an adult. My delivery has gotten slicker with years of practice, and the lines are uttered with greater glibness, but the story I often tell myself is still basically the same: "If I only had this, I would be completely satisfied."

No matter how quickly or completely we try to satisfy our wants, it never seems to be enough—new desires appear in place of the old ones, and again we feel unsatisfied. We spend our lives in the pursuit of satisfaction, of what we think will bring us happiness or self-esteem. It is a pattern that, as the story about my friends' children illustrates, becomes established early, and the stakes only get higher as we get older. The toys get more expensive and the search takes on a deeper tenor. We look for satisfaction in not only acquisition but also achievement, in not only what we have but also what we can do.

The transition in our search for satisfaction starts for most of us in high school or college. Those who are academically talented throw themselves into their studies, sometimes sacrificing everything else in the quest for a perfect GPA. Others delve into sports, or theater, or music. Some discover the opposite sex and dating and look for satisfaction through a relationship with another person. Others become part of a clique and derive satisfaction from belonging. Sometimes we find satisfaction in these things—for a while. But eventually we fail a test—or don't make the team—or don't get the part—or muff a recital—or have our affection spurned—or are left out of the "cool" crowd—and that which seemed to hold the promise of fulfillment becomes merely another disappointing exercise in futility. We are left unsatisfied and search for significance in something else.

When we have finished school, we pour ourselves into new pursuits: careers, ministries, advanced degrees, relationships. We grow older; the time remaining for us to make our mark on the world starts running out. Our biological clocks tick on toward some jangling, insistent biochemical alarm, and we see our opportunities for marriage and parenthood slipping past, like sand through the hourglass. The search for satisfaction goes on with no truly satisfying end in sight, and we begin to experience that sickening, penetrating fear that we will die unsatisfied, that those longings and yearnings will never be filled.

- "I'll never find someone to marry!"
- "I'll never have kids!"
- "I'll never be successful!"
- "I'll never become influential!"

This fear becomes despair, an unshakable feeling of help-less hopelessness and hopeless helplessness, a cancer of the spirit that appraises all that we have done, all for which we have striven as meaningless and insignificant. No ac-complishment is adequate to appease it. Thoreau said, "The mass of men lead lives of quiet desperation,"[2] and that is where this fear leads—to a quiet desperation. We fear that all of the time poured into our careers amounts to nothing. We fear that we will never find a mate and will spend the rest of our lives in loneliness. We fear that no matter where we direct our energies, no matter how well we do things, no matter how hard we try, no matter how good we are, *nothing* can satisfy us—and we know, because we have tried *everything*. We are drawn inexorably toward a most frightening conclusion—in the naïveté of our youthfulness all that we thought was good and satisfying turns out to be neither. What will satisfy us? Will anything?

I Can't Get No Satisfaction

Perhaps no one asked the question "What will satisfy me?" to greater effect than Solomon, Israel's third king af-ter Saul and David. He recorded his search for the answer in the Old Testament book of Ecclesiastes, which is tucked in between Proverbs and Song of Songs. You might never have heard it taught or read through it yourself because its tone can seem quite depressing. In fact, its skeptical atti-tude toward life caused it to be named one of the five "antilegomena"—books "spoken against" by some rabbis of old who didn't think that such pessimistic writings be-longed in the Old Testament.

Solomon ruled over a prosperous and politically stable king-dom. He had riches beyond imagination and numerous wives and concubines. Yet, in the guise of his alter ego, Qoheleth (the Preacher), he asked the same questions that we ask.

- "What will fulfill me?"
- "What will make my life meaningful?"
- "What am I looking for?"

It seems strange that someone like Solomon would ask such questions. He had everything; of all people, he certainly should have felt satisfied. But he did not. So he asked the question that we still ask some three thousand years later: "What will satisfy me?"

"If I Only Had a Brain . . ."

In Qoheleth's pilgrimage to find the source of satisfaction, he considers many possibilities. One is wisdom. Knowledge, intellectual prowess, acumen, insight, perspicacity—these are all qualities that are valued by our society and that most of us hold in high regard. Wisdom includes not only high intelligence but also the ability to apply that intelligence with common sense to the problems of life—to know what is best to do in all situations and circumstances.

You would think that having wisdom would be satisfying. After all, if I am smart, if I know many things, and if I can apply what I know to life, I should be able to make myself happy. To begin with, I should derive an innate pleasure from just knowing that I am wise (and knowing that others know it, too). In addition, I should be able to use my wisdom to acquire whatever else I think necessary to make me happy.

Was there ever anyone wiser than Solomon? Is it not Solomon's wisdom, perhaps more than anything else, for which he is most famous? The Queen of Sheba heard of Solomon's wisdom and came to see for herself. She concluded,

> "It was a true report which I heard in my own land about your words and your wisdom. Nevertheless I

did not believe the reports, until I came and my eyes had seen it. And behold, the half was not told me. You exceed in wisdom and prosperity the report which I heard. How blessed are your men, how blessed are these your servants who stand before you continually and hear your wisdom."[3]

Not surprisingly, then, Qoheleth recognizes that wisdom is a thing to be greatly prized, a thing that should bring him immense satisfaction, and he sets out to acquire it.

I set my mind to seek and explore by wisdom concerning all that has been done under heaven. . . . I said to myself, "Behold, I have magnified and increased wisdom more than all who were over Jerusalem before me; and my mind has observed a wealth of wisdom and knowledge."[4]

But despite having all of this great wisdom, what did Qoheleth conclude?

I set my mind to know wisdom and to know madness and folly; I realized that this also is striving after wind. Because in much wisdom there is much grief, and increasing knowledge results in increasing pain.[5]

Although it might seem otherwise while pulling an all-nighter on a take-home exam, the sad truth is that a perfect score will not satisfy you. Neither will a 4.0 GPA. Neither will the ability to discourse for hours on the subtleties of quantum mechanics or the works of Jane Austen. Even being able to quote Scripture at length from memory will not be satisfying if that is all Scripture is to you—something to be memorized and quoted to impress others. Wisdom will not provide ultimate satisfaction. Wisdom provides only what we might call "satisfiction"—the transitory illusion that you are satisfied, which lasts only until another want comes along.

"Party On . . ."

With wisdom out of the running, what else might satisfy us? Pleasure, perhaps? We all like to enjoy ourselves; everyone wants to have a good time. Solomon had access to more entertainment and pleasure than most of us. So what did Qoheleth do?

> I said to myself, "Come now, I will test you with pleasure. So enjoy yourself." . . . I provided for myself male and female singers and the pleasures of men—many concubines. . . . All that my eyes desired I did not refuse them. I did not withhold my heart from any pleasure.[6]

Having access to all of this entertainment, able to indulge in any pleasure, what did Qoheleth discover?

> And behold, it too was futility. I said of laughter, "It is madness," and of pleasure, "What does it accomplish?"[7]

Pleasure does not satisfy either. Partying your way through life, though fun for a while, will not provide true satisfaction. Pleasure, too, can provide only "satisfiction."

"Spend, Spend, Spend . . ."

With wisdom and pleasure discounted, what about wealth and possessions? What about accomplishment?

> I enlarged my works: I built houses for myself, I planted vineyards for myself; I made gardens and parks for myself and I planted in them all kinds of fruit trees; I made ponds of water for myself from which to irrigate a forest of growing trees.[8]

Quite a home improvement project, wasn't it?

> I bought male and female slaves and I had homeborn slaves. Also I possessed flocks and herds larger than all who preceded me in Jerusalem. Also, I collected for myself silver and gold and the treasure of kings and provinces. . . . Then I became great and increased more than all who preceded me in Jerusalem.[9]

I don't know about you, but the thought of owning slaves has never appealed to me (although having a full-time maid, cook, butler, and chauffeur might be nice!), and I have never had much interest in raising livestock. Gold, silver, treasure—those are things I can embrace with a bit more enthusiasm! But in Qoheleth's day, the symbols of wealth and power included not only gold and silver but also slaves, flocks, and herds. The symbols of wealth in our day may be different, but the point is the same. Qoheleth was seeking satisfaction in possessions, wealth, and the trappings of wealth. Did he find it?

> Thus I considered all my activities which my hands had done and the labor which I had exerted, and behold all was vanity and striving after wind and there was no profit under the sun.[10]

Although the world tells us that satisfaction is to be found in wealth, possessions, and power, they, too, provide only "satisfaction" and will not fill the void that we feel.

Tiny Bubbles

Qoheleth's first words in Ecclesiastes sound the theme that he develops again and again in specific cases: "Vanity of vanities! All is vanity!" The literal sense of the Hebrew word for vanity *(hebel)* is "breath" or "vapor."[11] It is the same word used in Proverbs 21:6: "The acquisition of treasures by a lying tongue is a fleeting vapor."

Someone suggested that a soap bubble was the perfect illustration of what this word means—after all, a soap bubble is nothing but an encapsulated breath. A soap bubble is pretty, it looks good, it is appealing—but it is also completely empty. Nothing substantial is inside it. Soap bubbles are fragile and easily broken. They float away on the wind—you reach out for them and they are gone; you touch them and they pop, dispersing the breath they enclosed. That same thought is expressed more poetically in an old Puritan prayer:

> Most men seem to live for themselves,
> > without much or any regard for thy glory,
> > or the good of others;
> They earnestly desire and eagerly pursue
> > the riches, honours, pleasures of this life,
> > as if they supposed that wealth, greatness, merriment,
> > could make their immortal souls happy;
> But, alas, what false delusive dreams are these!
> And how miserable ere long will those be that sleep in them,
> > for all our happiness consists in loving thee,
> > and being holy as thou art holy.
> O may I never fall into the tempers and vanities,
> > the sensuality and folly of the present world!
> It is a place of inexpressible sorrow, a vast empty nothingness;
> Time is a moment, a vapour,

and all its enjoyments are empty bubbles,
fleeting blasts of wind,
from which nothing satisfactory can be derived. . . .[12]

We spend so much of our lives chasing these empty bubbles that are buoyed up on the wind, striving after things that seem attractive and give the impression of being satisfying but that are really empty and meaningless. Eventually, we need to come to the same conclusion as Qoheleth:

Remember also your Creator in the days of your youth, before the evil days come and the years draw near when you will say, "I have no delight in them" . . . Remember Him before the silver cord is broken and the golden bowl is crushed, the pitcher by the well is shattered and the wheel at the cistern is crushed; then the dust will return to the earth as it was, and the spirit will return to God who gave it. . . . The conclusion, when all has been heard, is: fear God and keep His commandments, because this applies to every person.[13]

The wisest, wealthiest, most pleasured, most accomplished men who ever lived learned this from life: the things that God provides—wisdom, wealth, pleasures, and accomplishment—can be satisfying, but only when we recognize them as gifts from Him and only when it is He, the Giver, who is sought and not the gift itself.

The God-Shaped Void

Other notables have learned this lesson, too. Augustine, writing at the end of the fourth century A.D., complained to God, "I was anxious to get married, make money, and become famous, and you laughed at the whole business."[14]

But later in his life, the same man would say, "You have made us for yourself, and our hearts are restless till they find rest in you."[15]

Blaise Pascal, a seventeenth-century philosopher, theologian, and mathematician, came to the same conclusion. He is usually given credit for making the observation, oft-quoted in Christian circles, that "there is a God-shaped void in the heart of every man, which only God can fill." I cannot find this exact phrase in any of Pascal's writings; it appears to be a terse paraphrase of what we can confirm he actually did say. Although the paraphrase is glib and sticks in one's mind, his original recorded remarks are even more insightful:

> All men seek happiness. There are no exceptions. However different the means they may employ, they all strive towards this goal. . . . Yet for very many years no one without faith has ever reached the goal at which everyone is continually aiming. All men complain: princes, subjects, nobles, commoners, old, young, strong, weak, learned, ignorant, healthy, sick, in every country, at every time, of all ages, and all conditions. A test which has gone on so long, without pause or change, really ought to convince us that we are incapable of attaining the good by our own efforts. But example teaches us very little. . . .
>
> What else does this craving, and this helplessness, proclaim but that there was once in man true happiness, of which all that now remains is the empty print and trace? This he tries in vain to fill with everything around him, seeking in things that are not there the help he cannot find in those that are, though none can help, since this infinite abyss can be filled only with an infinite and immutable object; in other words, by God himself.[16]

If you are not married, if you are not in a serious relationship, if you are not even dating, and if you are unhappy with that state of affairs, it is tempting to believe that the thing missing from your life is the most obvious one: a spouse, a significant other, or simply a date on Saturday night. But failing to look beyond the obvious can put us back on the "satisfiction" merry-go-round—trying in vain to capture the brass ring of happiness. Getting married, or being in a steady relationship, or even finding someone to date will not bring lasting happiness, true fulfillment, and deep satisfaction. No human relationship can fill the void that can be filled only by God. We will find satisfaction only when we turn our unfulfilled desires over to God— when we seek Him above all else—when we finally stop looking to another person, or to the things of this world, or to the fruits of our own labors for fulfillment. Only when we turn to Him will the empty ache be cured.

We are blessed because we can see in retrospect what Solomon could only imagine in anticipation—the person of Jesus Christ, the one who enables Pascal's God-shaped void in our hearts to be filled. We need no longer feel an emptiness, a hunger—"I am the bread of life; he who comes to Me shall not hunger . . ."—or a thirst—"He who believes in Me shall never thirst"—or a weariness—"Come to me, all who are weary and heavy-laden, and I will give you rest." We need not feel like partial people, not yet whole because we still lack a mate—"In Him, you have been made complete."

Let us apprehend that truth—let us put aside all that is "vanity and striving after wind"—let us focus on Jesus and allow God to work out the processes of recasting us into the likeness of His Son. If we feel incomplete as single men and women, if we pine for a mate, or if we long for satisfaction in life, let us bring that need before Him in prayer, let us allow Him to use that longing to draw us closer to Him. But let our focus be on Him, allowing Him to show us that He is sufficient to meet that longing. And if He provides us with a partner, let us delight not only in the gift but also and foremost in the Giver; let our joy be not only in the provision but also and foremost in the Provider.

Consider This

1. What do you think that you are missing in life? Why do you think that having this thing will make you feel satisfied? What is it about this thing that you think will provide satisfaction?
2. What do you think might be God's purpose in not yet providing the thing that you think you lack?
3. Can you think of ways in which pursuing this thing draws you away from God? How can you ensure that you grow closer to rather than more distant from God?

chapter four

Gaining Wait

We must wait, wait, wait on the Lord
We must wait, wait, wait on the Lord
And learn our lessons well
In His timing He will tell us,
What to do, where to go, what to say.
—Randy Thomas,
"We Must Wait (On the Lord)"[1]

When I looked up the song above to verify the author and that I had remembered the words accurately, I dug out a slim volume bound with a black plastic spiral. On the cover, borders and ornaments made from musical symbols are placed on a background that resembles a handwritten score viewed through a kaleidoscope. *The Song Book* contains 129 of the favorite songs of a singles Bible study of which I was once a part. We had finally grown tired of our old song "books"—tattered collections of dog-eared, well-thumbed pages, some photocopied and some handwritten, some stapled into manila file folders and others simply stuffed in, relying on friction to keep them there—so we produced new ones that were made neat, orderly, and perhaps even beautiful through the modern miracle of desktop publishing.

As I held *The Song Book* in my hands and flipped through

it, all sorts of memories came flooding back. Memories of my friend Steve, the graphics whiz who designed the elegant cover. Memories of my friends Dieter and Ken and Laura, who strummed their guitars and led us in singing. Memories of the others in that group, all of our voices raised in songs of praise and worship. Memories of songs the strains of which I can still hear in my mind's ear, songs that evoke remembrances of a time, a place, and a group of people who figured significantly in my life before marriage.

I was single, just out of graduate school, starting a career as a research scientist. My church was the first church I'd found with teaching that didn't "dumb down" the Bible. Scripture was explained clearly and applied aptly, so that the truth revealed by the teaching stimulated my mind and then penetrated my heart. I was learning in a deeper and more personal way what it really meant to follow Christ, to live a life of sacrificial love, to strive to be a servant, and to be in committed fellowship with others. I had been blessed with several friends whom I met through various ministries of that church and who were at a similar stage in life. We felt that as "postcollege, premarriage Christians" we didn't really fit well into any of the established programs offered by our church at that time. So several of us had spontaneously formed a Bible study. Some of us were either still in or, as I was, just out of graduate school; others were already working in a variety of jobs: teachers, salespersons, ministry interns, and engineers.

When we first starting meeting, we were all single, most of us in our early- to mid-twenties. The group met regularly for about seven years, reckoned from the time it first got going to when it finally petered out. People came and went during that time, although a fair number of them lasted for the duration. When I close my eyes I can still see most of the faces, I can still picture clearly the places we met, and I can still hear the strains of the songs we sang.

Those songs ranged the gamut from Charles Wesley and John Newton to Twila Paris and Michael W. Smith, from "Great Is Thy Faithfulness" and "Holy, Holy, Holy" to "Seek Ye First" and "Be Ye Glad." But of all the songs that we sang, perhaps "We Must Wait" is the one that best captures both the promise and the struggle of those years. It crystallized both our anticipation that God had great things in store for us and our frustration over waiting on Him, rather than plowing ahead in our own eagerness and headstrong desire to make them happen.

And perhaps to no area of our lives was the song "We Must Wait" more applicable than our love lives. Most of us wanted to get married—if not right then, at least at some point in the future—and most of us did. Over the years, our group congregated at many weddings. I still remember the first such wedding. We sat outside on a beautiful spring day at the reception, all of us clotted together in a corner, rejoicing for the happiness of our friends but wondering who would be next and when our turns would finally come. Year by year, more of our number joined the ranks of the connubially blissful, and fewer of us were left among the waiting. But do you know what? Nearly fifteen years later, some of them are still waiting, still "learning their lessons well," still waiting for God in His timing to tell them "what to do, where to go, what to say."

The Waiting Game

What we sometimes call "the dating game" is equally well described as "the waiting game." Waiting seems to be an unavoidable part of the process: waiting for someone to ask you out, waiting to see if someone you've asked out will say "yes," waiting for someone in whom you are interested to stop dating someone else and become "available," waiting to see if the person you are dating is the one you want to marry, and waiting to see if the other person feels the same way.

But waiting is also something with which we have become increasingly intolerant. Perhaps that is because the technological innovations of the past century have accelerated life—or at least our expectations of how fast-paced life should be. Waiting now seems an archaic annoyance associated with the days of buggy whips and the Pony Express. We have come to resent being made to wait for anything; technology has created the expectation that we shouldn't have to wait. Fax machines, e-mail, and cell phones make it possible to send a message instantly to virtually any place on the globe. Automated teller machines enable us to do our banking whenever we please. Internet shopping makes it possible for us to quickly search for the best price on almost anything we want and to order it with the click of the mouse; express shipping puts it on our doorstep the next day. The mantra of our time has become "24/7"— whatever it is, we have access to it twenty-four hours a day, seven days a week. James Gleick's entertaining and thought-provoking book *Faster: The Acceleration of Just About Everything* contains the following quotation from a magazine editor that well illustrates modern impatience: "I can't stand small talk, waiting in line or slow numbers on the dance floor. . . . It has gotten to the point where my days, crammed with all sorts of activities, feel like an Olympic endurance event: the everydayathon. . . . I hear an invisible stopwatch ticking even when I'm supposed to be having fun."[2]

Waiting List

Scientific advancement and the acceptance of an accelerated pace of life have so accustomed us to immediate gratification that waiting now seems wrong, unproductive, and even personally insulting. In our action-oriented culture, waiting may also seem "passive" and "weak"; "strong" people aggressively go after what they want. But is that what Scripture teaches us about waiting? Without too much effort, we can think of several Bible characters who were forced to play the waiting game in one form or another.

- Abraham, married to a barren wife, waited twenty-five years for the fulfillment of God's promise to make him the father of a great nation, as numerous as the stars in the heavens.
- Jacob waited and worked seven years for a wife only to discover that he had been tricked and would have to work seven more years.
- Noah spent more than a year cooped up on a boat with a zoo full of animals, waiting for the waters of God's wrath to subside.
- Moses waited for Pharaoh to release the people of Israel, waited for them to accept their position as God's people, waited for them to learn obedience, and waited forty years sojourning in the wilderness as the disobedient generation perished so that Israel could enter the Promised Land. Despite all of that waiting, Moses never got to enter the Promised Land himself.
- Hannah, whose womb "the Lord had closed," waited "year after year" for a child, all the while being taunted and provoked by her fertile rival, Peninnah.
- David waited years after his anointing by Samuel to take the throne as king of Israel while enduring Saul's enmity.
- The Israelites in captivity in Babylon waited for God to restore them to their land.
- Nehemiah waited patiently for the right time and the opportune moment to return and rebuild the walls of Jerusalem.
- Jesus waited attentively on the Father for the right timing

of everything, saying at various times, "My time has not yet come," or "My time is not yet at hand."

We may look at these accounts with a certain dismay, deploring the colossal waste of time that attends some of them. In our day and age, at least some of the waiting described would be unnecessary. Surely the arrival of Abraham's progeny could have been hastened by the advances of modern reproductive medicine; surely Jacob's wait for a bride would have been mercifully shortened by modern sensibilities, labor laws, and drive-through wedding chapels. But is waiting bereft of any value whatsoever? Can we learn nothing from it? Can we derive no spiritual benefit from it? Doesn't the example of Jesus, exquisitely sensitive to the timing of His Father, offer us a clue that waiting might not be simply an annoyance that is to be avoided but something that is imposed for our ultimate benefit?

Why Do We Wait?

As Christians, we wait, not because there is no other alternative, but because waiting is the active practice of the faith that we profess. The writer of Hebrews says that "faith is the assurance of things hoped for, the conviction of things not seen."[3] What is waiting if not the anticipation of things hoped for? We wait, therefore, because faith requires waiting and, conversely, because waiting requires faith.

We wait, not because we are forced to wait but because waiting is the dynamic exercise of dependence and trust; it is the day-to-day demonstration of the obedience that we claim as our way of life. We wait in acknowledgment that we are not the ultimate author of our lives and that we submit to the sovereignty of Him who is our author. We wait on God's timing and upon His answer, contenting ourselves in the knowledge that He loves us and intends what is best for us. Men and women of faith have always waited thus on God's timing, as the "waiting list" above shows.

How Do We Wait?

Do we bite our fingernails, anxious over what God will do, how and when He will do it, and what its effect on us will be? Or do we wait expectantly, confident that God indeed loves us, certain that He keeps His promises, and eager to see how He will be pleased to act? Do we endure the wait in a manner that is consistent with the faith that we profess—with an assurance of things hoped for (such as His unsurpassed love for us) and with a conviction of things not seen (such as the exercise of His sovereignty and omnipotence in our lives)? Or do we endure the wait as though it were torture? Do we weep and moan and rail against God for unfairly taxing our patience?

Waiting Christians do not shut themselves up in closets, cutting themselves off from life, refusing to emerge until they see God act. A Christian who is waiting upon the Lord is a figure of faithful activity—praying, expectantly anticipating God's action, not obsessed with his or her own unfulfilled desires but looking beyond the horizon of personal need, ministering to the needs of others.

In the dating realm, many times of waiting may occur, but these times should not offer us license to become bitter, frustrated, and discontented. When no one is asking us out, when there is no one in our circle in whom we are interested, when we have decided to ask someone out and are waiting to see how that person will respond, when we are finally in a relationship and are waiting to see how it will develop, when we are waiting for whatever reason, our hearts should adopt an attitude of waiting expectantly on the Lord—confident, certain, and eager.

The story of Hannah provides insight into waiting and

deserves further examination. Her story is found in the book of 1 Samuel. Hannah was one of Elkanah's two wives. She was barren, but Elkanah's other wife, Peninnah, was fertile and bore him children. Hannah desperately wanted to have children, and Peninnah, apparently out of sheer meanness, continually taunted Hannah because she could not conceive. As one poet put it,

> She tried to put Hannah
> in her place
> instead of trying
> to put herself in Hannah's.[4]

Despite her barrenness and Peninnah's persistent sniping, Hannah had much about which to rejoice. She had a husband who loved her deeply. Some commentators have suggested that Hannah was probably Elkanah's first wife and that he took a second wife only after Hannah proved to be barren.[5] That this practice was permitted under Israelite law is suggested by Deuteronomy 21:15–17, which prohibits withholding an inheritance from the firstborn son of the "unloved" wife in preference to the first son born (later) of the "loved" wife. Perhaps it is not fair to label Peninnah as "unloved," but it is clear that Elkanah treated Hannah with special attention. First Samuel 1:5 tells us that on a feast day, Elkanah gave Hannah a "double portion" of the sacrifice, and we are told very specifically that it was because "he loved Hannah." He attempted to console her in her barrenness by pointing out that he was better to her "than ten sons." But an abundance of one good thing will not necessarily make up for the lack of another. Elkanah's abundant love did not reduce Hannah's longing for a child or her distress over not being able to bear one.

What was Hannah's response to her situation? Did she bear it stoically? No. In fact, we read in 1 Samuel 1:7 and 10 that she was greatly distressed, cried long and bitterly, and refused to eat. But ultimately, she got past the distress, past the tears, and past the bitterness, and she prayed. She asked God to look on her with favor and grant her a son—in fact, she promised to give that son back to God for His service. So fervent were her prayers that a priest watching her assumed that she was drunk! When questioned by the priest, she described her prayer as "an outpouring of my soul."

For single Christians, the question that drives us to bitter tears, emotional distress, and loss of appetite is not "when will You give me a son?" but "when will You give me a spouse?" (or at times even "when will You give me a date?") Yet we can still learn something from Hannah's situation. Do we focus on what God *hasn't* given us and neglect what He *has* given us? True, Hannah didn't have a child, but she did have Elkanah's love, which perhaps Peninnah did not. True, we might not have a mate, but what other blessings has God showered upon us?

Hannah was afflicted by a malicious tormentor who took delight in reminding her that she had what Hannah didn't have. To quote John Thomas Carlisle again,

> There is an unkind
> kind of exultation—
> the heartless gloating
> which Peninnah
> exhibited because—
> by chance or by providence—
> she could conceive
> easily and often.[6]

Single Christians might not be subject to the kind of "heartless gloating" that Peninnah dished out, but we are often reminded of what we lack. When others share with us their joy over getting asked out, getting engaged, or getting married, it often becomes "an unkind kind of exultation," even if not intended as such.

Despite our distress, whether inflicted externally or arising from internal dissatisfaction, are we able to get past the tears and get down to the business of praying as Hannah did? And when we do pray, do we do so perfunctorily or with a passionate and honest outpouring of our souls? Have any of us ever prayed so fervently that an onlooker would think we were intoxicated? And when our prayers are answered, are we willing to freely offer back to God for His service what He has given us?

How Long Do We Wait?

We singles, like the ancient Hebrews, can be an impatient and stiff-necked people. We worry that our lives are slipping away, that we don't have much time left to find a mate and get married. We desire to see God act immediately, and we start complaining when He does not. Hebrews 11 contains a long list of ancient Israelites who waited in faith for the fulfillment of God's promises. God promised Abraham that he would have an heir of his own blood. But how long was he then required to wait for that heir? How much time passed without Sarah's becoming pregnant? How long did Abraham struggle with doubt that there were too many obstacles and not enough time for God to fulfill His promise?

Abraham and Sarah got tired of waiting after a decade passed with no children. They decided that God needed some help in executing His plan, and so we read in Genesis 16 that Abraham impregnated Sarah's maid, Hagar, who bore him an heir named Ishmael. But did God really need such help? This incident poisoned the relationship between Sarah and Hagar, and many pundits trace the hostilities that still exist between the Jewish and Arab peoples of the Middle

East back to the birth of Ishmael. I wonder if there is a lesson for us in the incident with Hagar as we struggle with waiting for a mate. When we think that God is not acting, we are tempted to take matters into our own hands—to "put ourselves out there" more in an effort to find a mate, to choose activities and groups based on how they might enhance our chances of finding a mate, and to give higher priority "for a season" to attracting the interest of the opposite sex. But is that what God really wants?

God did fulfill His promise to Abraham, and at last Isaac was born of Sarah. That for which Abraham had waited so long was finally accomplished. But then God required Abraham to give back the fruit of his endurance. Abraham must have been tempted to succumb to bitterness and frustration, but he did not. Instead, he acted in faith and believed that God would honor His promise, even if he could not see how God would do so. In fact, it was not Isaac's life that God wanted but Abraham's heart—and that is what He wants of us, too. Are we willing to wait patiently for God's fulfillment of His promises to unfold? Are we faithful enough to hold loosely the blessings that He does grant us and offer them back to Him, willing to wait and see how He will act next?

God promised Abraham that he would have an heir produced out of his own body, and Abraham saw that promise fulfilled. But God also promised Abraham that his descendants would be "as the stars of heaven in number, and innumerable as the sand which is by the seashore."[7] Having just mentioned Abraham and this promise, the writer of Hebrews tells us that "all these died in faith, without receiving the promises, but having seen them and having welcomed them from a distance, and having confessed that they were strangers and exiles on the earth."[8] Abraham did not live to see this second promise fulfilled, yet he surely believed that it would be fulfilled, and he was willing to wait in faith for as long as it took.

How long do we wait? We wait as long as it takes, confident that God does fulfill His promises, even if we never live to see it.

Already, But Not Yet

If you think about it, waiting is really the default condition of the church and thus, by extension, the condition of each Christian whom the church comprises. We already know what will be the outcome of history—Scripture tells us—and we are waiting for God to bring it about. We are stuck in a kind of limbo between the "already" and the "not yet," between what God has already begun in restoring fallen man to his intended glory and right relationship with Him and what He has not yet brought to its full expression and final state. He has already made us new creatures, but we do not yet experience the full measure and manifestation of that new creaturehood. He has already cleansed us and made it possible for us to enter into His presence through the mediation of His Son, the perfect and acceptable sacrifice, but we do not yet experience His presence as intimately as we one day will. He has already achieved victory over and vanquished the foe, but the foe has not yet admitted defeat. In addition to whatever role modern technology may have played in increasing our impatience, we might find waiting difficult because we sense the tension between the "already" and the "not yet." We "groan within ourselves," Paul says, "waiting eagerly for our adoption as sons, the redemption of our body" just as "the anxious longing of the creation waits eagerly for the revealing of the sons of God" as it "groans and suffers the pains of childbirth together until now."[9] Labor has already begun, but the baby has not yet been delivered.

Thus, there is no pat answer to the question "How long do we wait?" We have no idea how long we might have to wait for a mate, just as neither Abraham nor Hannah had any idea how long they would be made to wait for children. God could bring potential spouses into our lives tomorrow—however, those persons may never come along. Is our faith strong enough to allow God sovereignty over that we which want so much and to which we ascribe such importance?

"Wait! Wait On! He Is Worth Waiting For!"

If I could travel back in time, one stop on my itinerary would surely be London, England, on Sunday, March 31, 1861. On that day, "the prince of preachers," C. H. Spurgeon, delivered his first message in the newly constructed Metropolitan Tabernacle. Only twenty-six years old, Spurgeon had been preaching in London for just seven years, but in that time his congregation had grown from about eighty to more than six thousand people. On that Sunday, the tabernacle was packed with something close to that number, seated on the main floor and in two galleries above. Their musical worship involved neither choir nor organ but thousands of voices raised in *a cappella* unison. What a sight and what a sound that must have been!

But perhaps the most lovely sound heard that morning was Spurgeon's own remarkable voice. Arnold Dallimore describes it thus in his excellent biography of Spurgeon:

> [H]is voice possessed not only a carrying quality but also an indefinable character that made many a hearer feel the preacher had singled him out and was speaking only to him. The voice was in perfect control, and though it could thunder with startling force it could also speak in the most moving, gentle tones. The phrase often used of it was "like a chime of silver bells."[10]

Unfortunately, Thomas Edison's invention of the phonograph was another sixteen years off, so we have today no way to experience Spurgeon's dulcet tones. However, something of the same charm and potency survives in his writing, which was prolific indeed. And somewhere in all of the countless words that he put to paper, Spurgeon had a few things to say about waiting, which are as apt now as they were a century ago:

> Wait in prayer. Call on God and spread the case before him. Express your unstaggering confidence in him. Wait in faith, for unfaithful, untrusting waiting is an insult to the Lord. Believe that if he shall keep you waiting even till midnight, yet he will come at the right time. Wait in quiet patience, not murmuring because you are under the affliction, but blessing God for it.[11]

Elsewhere, he wrote,

> God kept his Son waiting and he may very well keep you in like posture, for how long did you delay and cause the Lord of grace to wait on you?
> "But I cannot see how I am to be delivered."
> Wait.
> "Ah, this is such a heavy burden."
> Wait.
> "But I am ready to die under this terrible load."
> Wait! Wait on! He is worth waiting for! *Wait* is a short word, but it takes a deal of grace to spell out its full meaning, and still more grace to put it into practice. Wait, wait.
> "Oh, but I have been unfortunate."
> Wait.
> "But I have believed a promise, and it has not been fulfilled."

Wait, for you wait in blessed company. You may hear Jesus saying, "I waited patiently" (Ps. 40:1). He is teaching us to do the same by his gracious Spirit.[12]

Although technology might have exacerbated our dislike of waiting, the essence of that dislike has always been present in the human character—the saints of Spurgeon's day who were seated in the Metropolitan Tabernacle struggled with it no less than we do. Perhaps that is why God has been making us wait throughout human history, forcing us to learn to trust Him, to remain content in Him, to have faith in His promises. That is a lesson worth learning and a process worth enduring. The wait for a spouse will eventually end for most of us. And when it does we will find new arenas in which God makes us wait, teaching us that it is He, and not we, who is in control of all human history and of each human life. We who are so conscious of time must learn to wait on the One who created it and for whom "one day is like a thousand years, and a thousand years like one day."[13] He will not make us wait forever.

Consider This

1. In what circumstances is it hard for you to wait?
2. Can you think of a specific instance in which God required you to wait for something? For what? How long did you wait? What did you do during that time?
3. Read through the four Gospels and note the times when Jesus was required to wait on the Father. What principles regarding waiting can we draw from these instances?

chapter five

"Don't Make No Sense"

Obedience is the key to all doors; feelings come (or don't come) and go as God pleases. We can't produce them at will, and musn't try.
    —C. S. Lewis, *Letters of C. S. Lewis*

A friend once told me a story about the man that she had dated in college and the dorm in which he had lived. The dormitory building was several stories tall and had a central spiral staircase that left an opening in the middle. From any floor, there was a clear shot all the way down to the ground level, providing an excellent vantage point from which to attack an unsuspecting victim with a water balloon. She told me that frequent "water wars" occurred that left most of the ground floor drenched and covered with the latex shrapnel from exploded balloons.

The job of cleaning up the mess fell to a wizened old janitor who had worked for the university as long as anyone could remember. You might think that he would have seen it all—you might imagine that nothing that these rambunctious students could do would shock or dismay this old man. And yet, my friend said, time after time she saw the old janitor mopping up the water, shaking his head in disbelief, muttering "Don't make no sense . . . don't make no sense . . . don't make no sense." She commented on the irony of the situation: when we were in college, we thought of ourselves as adults and wanted to be treated as adults; yet we did things that in retrospect seem very juvenile. The term *adult* implies certain characteristic adult behavior; when one is called an adult but manifests unadult behavior, an obvious inconsistency exists. As the janitor quaintly put it, "It don't make no sense."

Similarly, calling oneself a "Christian" creates a certain expectation of behavior and belief that reflect the character of Christ. But the behavior of some single Christians in modern churches, singles groups, Bible studies, home fellowships, and even groups of Christian friends often leaves one shaking one's head in disbelief and muttering, "Don't make no sense." It "don't make no sense" that a Christian woman would choose to have a non-Christian boyfriend. It "don't make no sense" that a man who says that he is committed to the Bible's teaching on sexual purity would choose to sleep with a woman before marriage. It "don't make no sense" that a godly woman would "lead on" a man when there is no romantic interest in her heart but merely to ensure the continuation of male companionship. It "don't make no sense" that a godly man would choose which Bible study to attend based on how many attractive women attend it. It "don't make no sense" that Christians of both sexes manipulate each other's emotions to achieve their own ends. How we behave is the visible manifestation of what we believe, and behaviors like those cited make one wonder about the beliefs of the average single Christian.

Why is it that the behavior of many single Christians "don't make no sense"? Is it the objective that is faulty? Is something wrong with wanting to be married, with wanting to find another Christian for a mate, or with wanting to spend time with Christians of the opposite sex? Of course not. The desire to be married or even to be in a significant relationship is neither wrong nor sinful, so it is not the mere fact that single Christians wish to be married that "don't make no sense." But when finding someone to marry becomes more important than being obedient to God, when the desire to become a couple overrides the commitment to treat one another as brother and sister in the Lord, when self-esteem is derived not from one's position in Christ but from whether or not one is dating—then something is wrong.

The problem is not so much with the desire for marriage (yet how many Christians bring that desire before God with willingness to obey His direction?), but with the priority that one places upon it and the methods one uses to achieve it. For many Christian singles today the desire to be married, or at least to be dating, seems to have become more important than the desire to love and obey God, and serve Him in whatever condition—single or married, dating or not dating—He has chosen for us. The desire to draw near to another person often supplants the desire to draw near to God and know Him intimately. The near-term satisfactions of dating and the lifelong delights of marriage are perceived as more important than the eternal rewards of knowing and serving the ever-living God. Indeed, marriage is often seen as a prerequisite to serving God fully or to becoming complete as a Christian.

When wanting a relationship becomes more important than obedience to God, the temptation to do whatever it takes to satisfy that want can become overpowering. Outwardly, the appearance of Christian singles might be that of submission to the Lordship of Christ Jesus. Inwardly, however, many single Christians are struggling to achieve through their own efforts what they no longer believe God will give them through His grace. For instance, we now have "Christian singles bars" that serve only nonalcoholic beverages, play only Christian music, and offer an environment where only Christians can "pick up" other Christians. There are cruises designed exclusively for Christian singles. A recent newspaper article reported, "Singles are paying hundreds of dollars to Christian and Jewish dating services and making the rounds of events at . . . churches and synagogues to increase the odds of finding a religiously compatible partner. They are even attending services, ogling each other over prayer books instead of margaritas."[1]

The life of the Christian should be a process of becoming more and more like Christ. Our hearts should long for our lives to manifest His character. We should desire to act as He would in any given situation. We profess to love Him and follow Him, and it should be our deepest desire to be like Him. Yet, try as I might, I find it difficult to imagine Jesus behaving in any of the ways that we've described here. Jesus did what was obedient, regardless of whether or not it was expedient. Above all else, Jesus' life was one of utter obedience, and it behooves us to examine the degree to which obedience is characteristic in us as Christians.

As we strive for obedience, we must be careful not to accept obedience grudgingly as the price of salvation and wind up with a life of cranky devotion, devoid of joy or gratitude. As we shall see later, obedience not only is the response of a heart grateful for salvation but also the way by which we enter into rest—true rest—God's rest. As singles, obedience to God might seem to take us farther from the fulfillment of our desires for a spouse and a family, but in fact it provides the stable foundation that makes for successful dating relationships, happy marriages, and secure families.

Obedience Is Foundational

Jesus challenged His followers, "Why do you call me, 'Lord, Lord,' and do not do what I say?"[2] We, too, are often guilty of the same thing. Do we talk about "loving the Lord" and "serving the Lord" but fail to acknowledge His lord-ship in the most fundamental way of all: by simply obeying Him? In Luke 6 Jesus says,

> "I will show you what he is like who comes to me and hears my words and puts them into practice. He is like a man building a house, who dug down deep and laid the foundation on rock. When a flood came, the torrent struck that house but could not shake it, because it was well built. But the one who hears my words and does not put them into practice is like a man who built a house on the ground without a foun-dation. The moment the torrent struck that house, it collapsed and its destruction was complete."[3]

Jesus likens the life founded on obedience to a house with a foundation laid on bedrock. It is a house that can withstand the powerful forces of nature because it is rooted in something stronger still. In contrast, the life that is not founded on obedience is like a house built on a shallow foundation. When the torrent comes, that house is destroyed. We often like to portray our "houses"—that is, our lives— as being built well and sturdy above the surface. We are proud to point out the improvements, especially the new coat of paint or the new roof that everyone can see from the outside. But the beauty of the house is irrelevant if the foun-dation is not stable.

The stresses of singleness can often expose the shallow foundations of our own spiritual lives. When we are faced with not getting what we want—or not getting it when we want it—then we see whether the faith that we profess is built on rock or sand. When we are faced with giving up something out of obedience to God—like dating a non-Christian, or going too far physically—then we see how secure the foundation of our faith really is. Obedience is basic. If we are calling Jesus "Lord" but are not acknowledging His Lordship in the choices that we make and in the actions that we take, we are hypocrites indeed.

Obedience Is Volitional

Notice that Jesus says that the one who comes to Him, hears His words, and "puts them into practice" is like the man building his house on rock, and the one who hears His words and fails to put them into practice is like the man building his house on sand. Simply coming to Him and hearing Him is not enough; we must decide to obey Him, to make righteous choices, to select that which God offers over that which the world promotes. This is true of every aspect of our lives as Christians and is perhaps nowhere more true than of the choices we make in relation to one another as men and women. Obedience must be more important to us than expedience; doing what is right must be more important than getting what we want; glorifying God must be more important than satisfying self.

The kind of obedience that we are to cultivate requires a continual choosing of that which is godly and a continual rejection of that which is not godly. The making of righteous choices is both a means by which God creates a Christlike character in us and a manifestation of that character as it develops. As Paul says in Colossians,

> Since, then, you have been raised with Christ, set your hearts on things above, where Christ is seated at the right hand of God. Set your minds on things above, not on earthly things. For you died, and your life is now hidden with Christ in God. When Christ, who is your life, appears, then you also will appear with him in glory.[4]

Notice that our identity in Christ is expressed in the lifestyle that we adopt and the choices that we make. We are to set our minds "on things above, not earthly things." It does not say that our minds *will* be set on the things above; it says that we *must* set our minds on them. Obedience is an act of volition on the part of the believer, a constant cultivation of holiness that is energized by the indwelling power of the Holy Spirit. Obedience is a choice. We must be continually choosing to obey no matter how impractical, inefficient, or ineffective it seems.

Obedience Is Possible

Praise God for that! How miserable would be life and how cruel would be God if He required an obedience that was not possible for us to give. But obedience is possible, even though not humanly so—only by God's grace, by our union with Christ, and by the indwelling of the Holy Spirit is it possible for us to be obedient. It is true that no Christian makes righteous choices all of the time, and no Christian perfectly obeys God in every instance. But it is also true that before coming to Christ it was not even possible for us to do so with any consistency, whereas now that we have come to Him, it is possible. Paul's words to the Colossians point this out. He can exhort his readers to "set their hearts on the things above" only because of the fact that they "have been raised with Christ." That they can even hope to set their minds on the things above is possible only because their lives have been "hidden with Christ"— as have ours.

Peter also speaks of obedience as a choice that is empowered by our very identity in the Lord:

Therefore, prepare your minds for action; be self-controlled; set your hope fully on the grace to be given you when Jesus Christ is revealed. As obedient children, do not conform to the evil desires you had when you lived in ignorance. But just as he who called you is holy, so be holy in all you do; for it is written: "Be holy, because I am holy."[5]

This passage contains a promise as well as a proviso. God promises that we are ultimately to be holy, even as Christ Himself is holy. Think about it! That it can be done at all, and that God would deign to do it, truly surpasses understanding. But there it is—the promise has been made. However, the promise is accompanied by a proviso: we are to pursue righteousness. We are to be obedient, actively bending our minds and spirits to the task of remaining true to the Lord. We are actively to refuse capitulating to the sin to which we formerly were enslaved. We see again not only that obedience is mandatory but also that it is possible— possible because of the amazing grace of God.

Notice that Peter calls us to be holy in all of our behavior. Is dating to be excluded from this exhortation? How often, in our interactions with single Christians of the opposite sex, do we project the appearance of those who "set our hope fully on the grace of God" while actually setting our hope on whatever slick line or smooth maneuver will attract someone who we think is cute? How often do we persist in viewing relationships and dating from the ignorance of our pre-Christian mind-set, deciding what is permissible by the standards of the world rather than by the standards that God has set? If our lifestyle is to be one of obedience, obedience must penetrate every aspect of our lives. We cannot choose to be obedient only when it is easy or costs us nothing. Obedience must be a choice that we undertake in every aspect of our lives, recognizing that God's grace makes it possible for us to obey.

Obedience Is Costly

Making holy choices often means making hard choices. Sometimes obedience means giving up something greatly desired, perhaps without understanding why. Abraham must have felt this way, his knife poised to take Isaac's life. Why should God require me to give Him my son's life? he must have wondered. But God did not want Isaac's life—He wanted Abraham's heart. He wants our hearts as well, and giving them to Him might require surrendering something or someone we don't want to live without.

Do we direct our own lives, or are they under God's direction? Do we insist upon self-sovereignty, or have we yielded sovereignty over our lives to the Lord? We sometimes act as if the purpose of coming to Christ is having Him help us live our lives better rather than surrendering our lives so that He may live through us. The notion that union with Christ in His resurrected life implies union with Him in His death seems to be unappreciated among modern Christians. In Paul's words,

> Don't you know that all of us who were baptized into Christ Jesus were baptized into his death? We were therefore buried with him through baptism into death in order that, just as Christ was raised from the dead through the glory of the Father, we too may live a new life. If we have been united with him like this in his death, we will certainly also be united with him in his resurrection. For we know that our old self was crucified with him so that the body of sin might be done away with, that we should no longer be slaves to sin—because anyone who has died has been freed from sin.[6]

The price of new life is death. We rejoice that we are freed from sin and that Christ's death enables us to "live a new life," but sometimes forget that such freedom arises from the crucifixion of our "old self" with Him. Yet, the death of our former sinful identity and the concomitant gift of Christ's identity as our own is the very heart of the gospel—that is what should make us rejoice. It would be a poor gift, indeed, if God merely invigorated our puny lives. He goes unimaginably farther and gives us the very life of His Son. But, in exchange, "our lives" as such and our right to live them as we please are swept away. We are put to death that God might raise us to a new life, and the new life that we have belongs not to us, but to Him.

"You are not your own . . . you are bought with a price." My home church has engraved these words at the front of our sanctuary to provide a constant reminder of this central guiding truth of Christian identity. Although these words are true of every aspect of our lives as God's rescued children, Paul penned them in the context of unrighteous sexual behavior. And sometimes it is in that aspect of our dating lives that we find obedience to be most costly. It is hard to say no to physical indulgence, and many of us stumble in that area. But obedience is often costly in other areas as well—saying no to dating unbelievers, no matter how strong the attraction; hurting someone's feelings and losing a friendship by rejecting a romantic advance; choosing a ministry that will glorify God and bless the body but reduce our chances of finding a mate; watching all of our friends getting married and wondering why God has left us single. Obedience is costly. But the price that God paid to establish a relationship with us—wherein it is even possible for us to be obedient—was costlier still.

Obedience Is Distinctive

"Don't make no sense" is a proper response when no apparent difference exists between the dating behavior of

Christians and that of non-Christians. However, the expected difference should spring not from a set of rules defining "holy dating" but rather from the hearts of Christians being focused on their Lord, whereas the heart of non-Christians are focused on themselves. We do not alter our behavior to prove that we are different from the world but rather we ourselves have been altered by the grace of God in such a way that different behavior results. If we are truly following Christ, the way we interact with each other as Christian men and women in the pursuit of matrimony will be fundamentally different from the way of the world. Our interactions will, out of love for and obedience to God, focus on the welfare of the other person rather than on the welfare of ourselves. That is why it "don't make no sense" to see Christian singles treating each other shabbily as they date. Our actions betray the true attitudes of our hearts no matter what we say with our mouths.

In his letter to the Ephesians, Paul says,

> So I tell you this, and insist on it in the Lord, that you must no longer live as the Gentiles do, in the futility of their thinking. They are darkened in their understanding and separated from the life of God because of the ignorance that is in them due to the hardening of their hearts. Having lost all sensitivity, they have given themselves over to sensuality so as to indulge in every kind of impurity, with a continual lust for more.[7]

Consider applying Paul's statement to the area of relationships. Is it not a fair description of the modern secular view (and, tragically, of some parts of the church) that commitment is frivolous and archaic; that how quickly a couple gets into bed is the measure of the vibrancy of a relationship; that it is acceptable to manipulate someone else's emotions to meet one's own needs; that a person's worth is determined by beauty, wealth, power, or charm? Is that what Christian relationships should be?

Paul continues,

> You, however, did not come to know Christ that way. Surely you heard of him and were taught in him in accordance with the truth that is in Jesus. You were taught, with regard to your former way of life, to put off your old self, which is being corrupted by its deceitful desires; to be made new in the attitude of your minds; and to put on the new self, created to be like God in true righteousness and holiness.[8]

We are to be very different indeed. Apply this description to the area of relationships. Do we "choose to refuse" to act in accordance with our old identities, the ones that were enslaved to sin and disregarded righteousness? Are we, as unmarried Christians, putting off the "old self," the one characterized by "deceitful desires" and leading to corruption? Perhaps these "deceitful desires" include those that seem to impel us toward unrighteous behavior in relationships—the desire to be valued by another person because we are deceived into thinking that our significance lies there; the desire to have what others have because we have been deceived into thinking that if only we had it, we would be happy, too; the desire for sexual experience because we have been deceived into thinking that it, by itself, will be fulfilling; even the desire for marriage, if we have been deceived into thinking that it will make us complete. Or are we embracing the "new self"? Are we choosing to live according to the new identity that our union with Christ makes possible? Are we allowing God to make us righteous and holy?

If obedience is indeed distinctive, and we have just seen

what the Christian community should not look like, we must ask the converse question: What should it look like? How are we to treat one another as brothers and sisters in the Lord? How are we to act on the basis of our identity in Christ? Consider Paul's words in his letter to the Philippians:

> If you have any encouragement from being united with Christ, if any comfort from his love, if any fellowship with the Spirit, if any tenderness and compassion, then make my joy complete by being like-minded, having the same love, being one in spirit and purpose. Do nothing out of selfish ambition or vain conceit, but in humility consider others better than yourselves. Each of you should look not only to your own interests, but also to the interests of others.[9]

The Greek words that Paul uses suggest that his *ifs* are rhetorical—that is, they do not express uncertainty over whether or not we actually have these things but imply that we already do have them, or should. We should have encouragement from our union with Christ, we should have comfort from his love, we should have fellowship with the Spirit, we should have tenderness and compassion, and these things should be made manifest in the way we treat one another.

The way we ought to treat one another is simply expressed, if not always simply executed: we humble ourselves and place the interests of others above our own interests out of love, being obedient to the command of our God, even as our Lord "did not consider equality with God something to be grasped, but made himself nothing, taking the very nature of a servant, being made in human likeness. And being found in appearance as a man, he humbled himself and became obedient to death—even death on a cross!"[10] That is the kind of humility that we need to adopt in dealing with each other—humility that is expressed in obedience even unto the death of our own dreams, our own desires, and our own selfish ends. That is the love of Christ, and that is the love with which we are privileged to love one another as His followers.

That is a very general statement of how we are to treat one another as members of the body of Christ. Scripture also offers us some specifics that are worth pondering. We are to

Be devoted to one another in brotherly love.[11]

Honor one another above yourselves.[12]

Live in harmony with one another.[13]

Stop passing judgment on one another. Instead, make up your mind not to put any stumbling block . . . in your brother's way.[14]

Pursue the things which make for peace and the building up of one another.[15]

Accept one another.[16]

Serve one another in love.[17]

Bear one another's burdens.[18]

Be kind and compassionate to one another, forgiving each other.[19]

[Cease lying] to one another.[20]

Bear with each other and forgive whatever grievances you may have against one another.[21]

Let the word of Christ richly dwell within you, with all wisdom teaching and admonishing one another with psalms and hymns and spiritual songs.[22]

Comfort one another.[23]

Encourage one another and build up one another.[24]

Consider how to stimulate one another to love and good deeds.[25]

[Cease speaking] against one another.[26]

Confess your sins to one another, and pray for one another.[27]

Fervently love one another from the heart.[28]

Be hospitable to one another without complaint.[29]

Clothe yourselves with humility toward one another.[30]

By Obedience, We Enter into God's Rest

The writer of Hebrews encourages his readers: "See to it . . . that none of you has a sinful, unbelieving heart that turns away from the living God."[31] To present an illustration of his argument, he reminds his readers of the Israelites, whom Moses led out of captivity. Of them he says,

Who were they who heard and rebelled? Were they not all those Moses led out of Egypt? And with whom was he angry for forty years? Was it not with those who sinned, whose bodies fell in the desert? And to whom did God swear that they would never enter his rest if not to those who disobeyed? So we see that they were not able to enter, because of their unbelief.[32]

The Israelites were not allowed to enter into God's rest because of their unbelief and disobedience. But, fortunately for us, "the promise of entering his rest still stands"[33] and "there remains, then, a Sabbath-rest for the people of God."[34]

What is the nature of this rest? The writer of Hebrews says that "anyone who enters God's rests also rests from his own work, just as God did from his."[35] By obeying God, we enter into a rest that results from being utterly dependent on Him, relying on His activity and agenda rather than our own. In the context of singleness, maybe this means depending on Him rather than on our own efforts to provide a mate. Maybe it means being willing to follow Him wherever He leads, even if the path that He chooses seems to take us farther away from marriage. Maybe it means being willing to step out in faith and assurance when He closes the door on a relationship. Perhaps the anxiety and frustration that we feel when our plans don't work out as we wished would dissolve into the peace of Sabbath-rest if only we would rest from our own work, if we would not try so hard to make things happen as we wish and when we wish, and if we would allow God to do what He does best—change lives and bless His children.

It is not always easy to act in obedience to God, especially when dating, love, romance, and sexual attraction are involved. It is not always easy, but it is obedient. And perhaps it is time for us to recognize obedience as the quintessential expression of our faith—we obey, not because we hope to gain from it, but because it is the proper response of a heart that trusts in God. Instead, the world has programmed us for expedience. We desire to have what we want, when we want it. But we must supplant the desire for expedience with the desire for true obedience. Unless our lives are founded in the willingness to obey, unless our relationships are founded in this sacrificial Christian love, and unless we as Christian men and women learn to treat each other first as brother and sister in the Lord, any more intimate relationship for which we might hope will ultimately be unfulfilling and unhealthy. All other relationships grow out of this: that we love first and most fervently the One who has saved us and set us free. It begins with a choice—a choice to serve Him rather than to serve ourselves; a choice to do what is obedient, even if by doing so we forfeit what we desire; a choice to pursue righteousness, even when it is costly. Are we willing to make that choice?

Consider This

1. What limits my willingness to obey God? Is it lack of clarity about what He wants me to do? Fear on my part of doing what He asks? Something else?

2. From a secular point of view, obedience is often seen as limiting or grudgingly given to a resented authority figure. How is obeying God different?

3. Using a concordance, examine Old and New Testament verses listed under *obey* (and forms thereof, such as *obeying, obeyed,* etc.), and *obedience.* Can you discover any aspects of obedience that were not discussed in this chapter?

chapter six

The Yoke's on You

Two beasts are bound with common yoke,
A heavy load to bear.
If oxen both, or donkeys both,
The burden they can share.

They draw the load with common force,
They step with balanced gait.
They walk in steady partnership,
Each equal with its mate.

But what if ox and ass are joined
And made to share the load,
Both yoked together, two-as-one,
To journey down the road?

The ox's greater stride and strength
The donkey cannot match.
The yoke that binds the two as one
Begins to wear and catch.

Each beast itself could do the job
If yoked with its own kind.
When bound with one of different breed
The yoke will chafe and bind.

The lesson of the ox and ass
Is one that should ring true.
Consider well your partner's heart
Before the yoke's on you.

—S. W. Irlee

Linda cleared her throat and slowly raised her hand.[1] It wasn't necessary to raise your hand to speak in our small singles Bible study. Most of us had met together long enough that we felt comfortable blurting out what we wanted to say during our sharing time. But Linda attended only occasionally, and perhaps she felt that this gesture was required to gain the floor politely. With everyone's attention focused on her, she began to share her story.

She asked for prayer for her relationship with her boyfriend, who was not a Christian. She shared that they were having problems in their relationship as a result of their religious differences. She felt that if she could only convince him to accept Christ, these problems would disappear and they could get married and be happy together. But for now, at least, he seemed to be indifferent to the truth of God, and his indifference was tearing her apart.

When Linda had finished sharing her story, we spent some time praying for the two of them. We bowed our heads together, and various people, as they felt led, prayed for her and for her boyfriend. It was a rich time when we were able to "bear one another's burdens,"[2] "pray for one another,"[3] and "comfort one another."[4] I felt honored that Linda had opened up to us, making herself vulnerable before her brothers and sisters in Christ, and the group was happy to lift up her concerns in prayer before the Lord.

But later, as I drove home and reflected upon the evening, I found myself plagued by conflicting thoughts. On one hand, I had no doubts that it was good to pray that Linda's boyfriend come to know the Lord. It was also good to pray that

Linda trust God for her relationship and to ask that her troubled heart be comforted.

On the other hand, I felt that our response to Linda's situation could be construed as tacit approval of a situation that was scripturally disobedient—a Christian woman dating a non-Christian man. Were we wrong, I wondered, to pray for God to change the young man's heart without asking Him to help Linda search her own heart concerning the wisdom of this relationship? Were we wrong to ask God to bail Linda out of a situation that resulted from her own unwise choice?

Rather than simply praying that Linda get what she wanted, would it not have been more loving to take another approach— encouraging her to study the Scriptures that speak about intimate relationships between Christians and non-Christians, then praying with an open heart about whether or not it pleased God for her to be in this relationship?

As I drove on that night, it struck me that we often accept sin and disobedience in our lives and pray for the lessening of its consequences, rather than praying for hearts that choose obedience instead. Yes, we are told to bear one another's burdens, to pray for each other, and to comfort one another, but we are also told to "[speak] the truth in love"[5] and to "consider how to stimulate one another to love and good deeds."[6] Linda's situation was not unusual. Before that night and since then, I've watched others struggle through such relationships. Caught up in the thrill of a new and exciting romance, even committed Christians find themselves putting their beliefs on the shelf for a time. But is that what God desires for us?

The Warning of the Word

Scripture, when appraised without the "that's not what I want to hear so I'm not going to listen" attitude, is pretty clear in what it says about intimate relationships between Christians and non-Christians. Few believers would argue that Scripture teaches that marriage between Christians and non-Christians is unwise even if they would not call it disobedience or sin. Most of us have read or been taught what the apostle Paul says in 2 Corinthians:

> Do not be bound together with unbelievers; for what partnership have righteousness and lawlessness, or what fellowship has light with darkness?[7]

The words *bound together* are rendered in other translations as

- "yoked together" (NIV)
- "mismated" (RSV)
- "unequally yoked" (KJV)
- "diversely yoked" (Darby)

Of these, I think that the *Revised Standard Version*'s "mismated" and *Darby*'s "diversely yoked" come closest to capturing Paul's thought. In trying to understand his meaning, it is helpful to go back to the underlying Greek text. Paul uses a very unusual Greek word—transliterated into English it is *heterozygountes*. You probably recognize the first part of this word—*hetero*. This prefix can be found in several English words, including *heterosexual, heterodox,* and *heterogeneous*. If you know any of these words, you can probably guess that the prefix *hetero* means "other." A heterosexual relationship is one between a person and a member of the other sex. A heterodox opinion is one that is other than the established view. A heterogeneous mixture is one in which one substance is mixed with some other substance.

We are not as familiar with the *zygountes* part (the form you would look up in a Greek dictionary is *zygeo,* which I will use from this point), but it means "to join, bind, or yoke." A few English words are derived from this root, but they are less familiar to most of us than *hetero*. (An exception is the word *zygote*, which you might recall from high school biology class. A zygote is the fertilized cell that results from the joining together of a sperm and egg.)

Zygountes evokes a picture from another place in Scripture, perhaps one that Paul had in mind when he wrote this passage. In the Septuagint (the translation of the Old Testament from Hebrew into Greek) the word *zygeo* is used by Moses in Deuteronomy 22:10: "Do not plow with an ox and a donkey yoked together" (NIV). Here, *zygeo* (without the *hetero* prefix) is used to describe the yoking together. Moses is addressing the Israelites, who are finally about to enter the Promised Land. This is the second generation after the Exodus from Egypt; the first generation was not allowed to enter the land because they did not have faith that God could indeed deliver the land into their hands. Moses was not allowed to enter the land either as the result of a different act of disobedience. Thus he needed to present the Law to this second generation and to give them some final instructions before Joshua led them into the land.

With all of the important things that Moses had to tell them, why did he worry about plowing instructions? His statement probably seemed as strange to the Israelites as it does to us. But none of them had ever plowed a field—this is the second generation, remember, and all they had ever known was wandering in the desert. Now they were about to enter a land where they would ultimately become farmers. They were going to enter the land, conquer it, and live there. They needed to know how to survive. Moses' instruction was intended to help equip them for that purpose.

It is unlikely that many of us have ever plowed a field— even more unlikely using draft animals. But in some places oxen and donkeys are still used for this purpose, and some people have studied these practices and understand them well. One such person is Drew Conroy, an Assistant Professor of Applied Animal Science at the University of New Hampshire and a modern-day "oxhandler extraordinaire." His teams of oxen have appeared in the movie *The Crucible* and in the television special *In Search of the Oregon Trail.* He has done extensive research in parts of the world where draft animals are still used much as they were in biblical times.

Professor Conroy told me that both oxen and donkeys are still used in parts of Africa for pulling plows, and when there is no alternative they are occasionally used together, though they are very different creatures. Oxen weigh more, but pound for pound, donkeys are actually stronger. Donkeys can survive on less water and pace themselves better, refusing to work when they become too tired. However, the main problem in using an ox and a donkey together is in finding a harnessing system that works well for both of them. "When donkeys are put in an ox yoke," Professor Conroy explained, "the animals cannot work. Donkeys hold their heads up; oxen hold their heads at the same level as their backs or lower. Oxen have a hump on their backs that a crude wooden yoke can ride against—if this yoke were used on a donkey, it would choke the animal."

The different anatomy of the two beasts makes it difficult to yoke them together in a way that is comfortable for both animals and allows them both to work at their full potential. To force a donkey to work in a yoke designed for an ox would not only reduce its effectiveness but also cause damage and pain. Moses' instruction not to yoke an ox and a donkey together was intended to impart blessing and avoid pain. If the Israelites obeyed his directive, they would be able to till their fields efficiently, and their animals would not be made to suffer unnecessary discomfort. A "silly rule" that might have seemed strange and completely arbitrary to the Israelites was really rooted in God's love for them; it was part of His provision to see them flourish in the Promised Land.

In writing about yoking a believer with an unbeliever, Paul could have simply used the word *zygeo* by itself, but instead he chose to coin the term *heterozygeo*. This word is intriguing. In all of the seventy million words of Greek literature surviving from ancient times, this word is used only about fifty times, and most of these occurrences are quotations of or comments upon Paul's writings.

Why did Paul tack on the *hetero?* Perhaps he wanted to emphasize that his objection to the relationship between a Christian and a non-Christian was the "otherliness" of the yoking, the fact that it joined two such dissimilar partners. There is nothing inherently wrong with the joining together of two creatures; there are some things that one creature simply cannot accomplish by itself. What Paul objects to is the disparity and utter dissimilarity between the creatures that are joined.

The Old Testament picture of joining an ox and a donkey helps convey this "otherliness" and illustrates the kind of partnership against which Paul is warning. Intimate association between a Christian and a non-Christian is an "otherly yoking," the pairing of two completely different entities. The result will likely be pain and a thwarting of God's plan for growth—destructive, and not productive as God intended. God sets those relationships off-limits, not according to some arbitrary whim but because He wishes to see us flourish. He is not being mean or restrictive but is demonstrating His love for us by preventing us from doing something foolish. Like a father warning his child to stay away from a hot stove, God's warning is a manifestation of His compassionate love for us.

The Rule for Relationships

The Meaning for Marriage

It is easy to see, then, how Paul's words should shape our view of romantic relationships. It seems clear, for example, that a Christian's entering into a marriage with a non-Christian is unacceptable in God's sight. Such a marriage is a lifelong yoking of dissimilar creatures. It is a union of two totally different beings—one who is alive to God and one who is dead to Him; one who is freed from bondage to sin and one who is still in captivity; one who is in the world but not of it and one who is worldly. How can someone whose heart belongs to God desire to be joined to someone whose heart rejects Him? How can someone who speaks the name of Jesus with love and reverence be bound for a lifetime to someone who uses His name only as a curse? If our hearts are truly committed to loving and serving Jesus, it seems incredible to consider marrying someone whose focus is not the same. It would be like buying a particular kind of car because it is a pretty color even though it doesn't have an engine. A Christian and a non-Christian do not even have the same basis for evaluating their relationship. As Paul says in 1 Corinthians 2:14,

> The man without the Spirit does not accept the things that come from the Spirit of God, for they are foolishness to him, and he cannot understand them, because they are spiritually discerned.[8]

A Christian married to a non-Christian makes no more sense than an ox yoked to a donkey.

The Difficulty with Dating

But what about dating? Many Christians who agree that

marriage between Christians and non-Christians is foolish and disobedient would not say the same about dating. After all, the level of commitment is very different. Anyway, what counts or doesn't count as dating? The line between "spending time together as friends" and "dating" often seems blurred. Most Christians have non-Christian friends; they work with them, spend time with them, enjoy their company, maybe even have opportunities to share the gospel with them. And aren't we called to be "in the world" even though we are not "of it"?[9] What is so terrible about casually dating a non-Christian?

The difficulty centers on what we mean by *dating.* This word can, and very often does, mean different things to different people. It can even mean different things to two people who are "dating" each other! I think of a female friend of mine who once told me she was "dating." She was seeing a man whom she did not find particularly attractive and in whom she had no real romantic interest, but he was willing to take her out to concerts, plays, dinners, and so forth. To her *dating* meant a man and a woman platonically enjoying social events together. At the other extreme—because of our culture's preoccupation with sex—*dating* is used to describe a relationship that involves little more than hopping into bed. However, I think that most people would describe dating as a process by which two people who feel some romantic attraction toward each other and who enjoy each other's company spend time together, get to know one another, and determine whether their relationship has the potential to grow into something more serious, committed, and intimate.

Our thinking about dating is further clarified if we realize that only two types of long-term relationships can exist between a man and a woman who are not blood kin: friendship and marriage. Dating is inherently a "metastable" relationship—it can last for a while, but it cannot persist indefinitely.

No one dates someone for life. Once you start dating a person, there are only two possible outcomes—either you will break up at some point, or you will wind up married. Dating is a process for determining whether or not a friendship has the potential for growing into a marriage; it is not an end in itself. It is a pathway from friendship to marriage, not the ultimate destination.

With this perspective, it is not hard to come to a conclusion about Christians dating non-Christians. If marriage between a believer and a nonbeliever is a yoking against which Scripture counsels, and if dating is trying on a particular yoke to see how it fits, then the same principle that governs our thinking about marriage should also apply to dating. If Christians are not to marry non-Christians, then there is little point in Christians dating non-Christians. To do so skirts the edge of disobedience, making subtle distinctions in what God has commanded us to do and not to do. That might be the way that lawyers approach the law and that politicians approach the truth, but it should not be the way that Christians approach their relationship with their Lord.

When we desire certain things more than we desire true obedience to God, we run the risk of spiritual disaster. We tread the boundary between what is godly and what is not, making choices that will both give us what we want and allow us to justify our choice as being spiritually sound. We may claim, for example, that dating a non-believer is a "witnessing opportunity." We say that we want to be good Christians and to grow in our relationship with the Lord, but when push comes to shove, we don't really want to sacrifice our own desires to accomplish that end. Shouldn't that give us cause for concern? Would we rather compromise integrity and personal righteousness than give up something that we want?

It is not easy to deny ourselves something that we greatly desire, especially in the area of romance. Our emotions and hormones send strong messages to our brains, and it is difficult to set those messages aside and make an intellectual decision—to say "I have a strong opinion about this, but I am not going to act in accordance with those feelings because I know it would not please God."

But guess what? Nobody ever said that the Christian life would be easy! If anything, we are promised that it is a hard and narrow road, one that not many people choose to follow all the way to the end. But the essence of becoming more Christlike is that we sort the conflicting inputs from intellect and emotion and choose that which is in accord with the Spirit of God. Choosing disobedience is wrong, no matter how strongly our emotions tell us to do so or how weakly our intellect protests. We can dance around the issue indefinitely, rationalizing our choices to the nth degree. But wrong is wrong. Sin is sin. Disobedience is disobedience. And no amount of slick talking or weasel wording changes that.

The Sounds of the Skeptic

I know that some people object to this conclusion. They point to specific examples where the "flirt-to-convert" approach has worked, where an unbeliever has, in fact, come to faith through a dating relationship with a believer.

Such examples do exist. I recently read a letter from Carol, a young, single Christian woman who was attracted to a non-Christian man and wanted to have a relationship with him. Carol was writing to Joan, another woman who, when a non-Christian, dated a Christian man and had eventually come to faith during the course of that relationship. Carol wanted reassurance from Joan that it was valid and acceptable to enter into a relationship with a non-Christian man, that an "otherly" yoking could work out and have a happy ending.

There is a danger in this type of thinking, in which we take an example of what can happen by God's grace and try to make it the norm. God may redeem bad choices, but He does not condone them or encourage them. If God in His sovereignty takes a disobedient, sinful situation in someone else's life and turns it around for His glory, does that give us license to indulge in the same disobedient act? Paul spends a lot of time in Romans arguing that the effectiveness of God's grace is not an inducement to further sin, and he comes to an emphatic conclusion: "What shall we say, then? Shall we go on sinning so that grace may increase? By no means!"[10]

Even if there are cases where by God's grace a nonbeliever comes to faith by dating a believer, far more often it is the believer's viewpoint that is changed and the believer's faith that is challenged. Regarding the story above, Joan related that her unbelief had weakened her Christian boyfriend's relationship with the Lord for a time and had led him away from the church and prayer. She also told of another friend whose walk with the Lord had been totally devastated as a result of a prolonged relationship with a non-Christian woman.

It is a fine and spiritual thing to desire that someone be led into relationship with Christ. But the process by which one is brought to faith is far better conducted in an environment that is less emotionally charged than is a dating relationship, in an atmosphere that does not have mixed motives and raging hormones built in. If those who "flirt to convert" seriously claim that winning others to Christ is their primary motivation, they must explain why the romantic element is necessary. If your purpose is to persuade this person toward Christ, why can't you do so in a non-dating context, with the participation of other believers and as brother and sister in the Lord, which is the relationship that you say you hope to achieve?

When a Christian is dating a non-Christian and other Christians express concern about the wisdom of such a relationship, this concern is sometimes perceived as an attack on the character of the non-Christian. A typical response might be, "But he [or she] is a fantastic person! I resent the suggestion that there is something wrong with him or that he is somehow less worthy or less valuable just because he is not a Christian!" Of course, this argument is perfectly true. Someone who does not know the Lord is not to be less valued or considered less worthy than someone who does know Him. We are all sinners who stand restored in God's sight only through identification with His Son, by His grace. But this objection misses the point of Paul's prohibition, and that is why attention should be paid to Paul's use of the word *heterozygeo*. The idea of "otherly" yoking is perhaps a better translation than the more traditional "unequal" yoking. The word *unequal* implies a scale by which value and worth are weighed. The word *other* makes clear that what Paul is considering is not a difference in value or worth but in kind. The objection to yoking is not because one animal is better or more valuable than the other—we pointed out earlier that both oxen and donkeys have their strong points—but because they are of two entirely different and incompatible varieties.

Others may raise the objection that the view of dating given here is too narrow, that it is harmless for a Christian and a non-Christian to spend time together as a couple, to go out together and not worry about their conflicting views unless they get serious enough to consider marriage. But, again, this argument tries to play lawyer with God's instructions. If the two people involved identify themselves as a "couple," if their relationship contains the elements that characterize most modern romantic relationships, if there is clearly a preference for doing things together as a couple rather than in a group, then a line has been crossed and a kind of yoking has taken place. The Christian in that situation would do well carefully and honestly to consider the following questions: What is this relationship really all about? If it isn't moving toward marriage and has gone farther than friendship, where now can it go? What desires does it satisfy, and do you really believe that this is a spiritually sound way to meet these desires? Does this relationship really strengthen and deepen your walk with the Lord? Does it edify and build you up in your faith? When dating is simply a way of meeting one's needs for companionship, social activity, self-esteem, or sex, all too often at least one of the partners involved winds up disappointed, disillusioned, or devastated.

The Rest of the Story . . .

I never learned what finally happened to Linda, the woman from our Bible study group for whom we prayed. She returned to our study after that night, but I don't recall her sharing anything more about their relationship. Eventually, she drifted out of our sphere, and I never found out how the rest of the story unfolded. But I've heard her story again, the same plot with different players. I've heard other stories, too: Christian sisters who date non-believers because Christian men do not ask them out; Christian brothers who date and marry only gorgeous women who ignore or abhor the things of God; fellow believers of both sexes who throw away their walks with the Lord for relationships that never had a chance because of the unbelief of their partners.

Do we love God? Are we willing to do what He asks simply because He asks it, taking it on faith that what He asks must ultimately be right? Are we willing to adopt a perspective that looks beyond the immediate horizon of what we want and catches a glimpse of what God desires to give? To some people, dating a non-Christian might seem a trivial thing that has little impact on one's faith. But little steps of disobedience and disregard for God's Word have a way of taking one a frightfully long way from where one wants to be. In ancient times, sailors always kept the shore in sight to ensure that they did not get lost. We would do well to do likewise as we navigate the often-treacherous waters of singleness and dating.

Consider This

1. Have you ever been in an "otherly yoked" relationship or attracted to someone who did not share your beliefs? What did you decide to do, and what did you learn from that experience? How, if at all, has the material in this chapter changed your view of such relationships?
2. Suppose that your best friend (a Christian) comes to you, bubbling over with excitement about the person he or she has just begun dating. As your friend tells you about this relationship, it becomes evident that this new person is not a Christian. How would you respond? Would you share their excitement without raising the issue of whether such a relationship is wise? How can you tell someone gently and with love that you think they are doing something disobedient in God's sight?
3. What other kinds of relationships do you think might fall under Paul's prohibition of "otherly yokings"? How are they different from or similar to dating and marriage?

chapter seven

A Commotion of Emotions

I want to do whatever's right,
But thought and feeling strive and fight.
While reason slowly weighs the choice
Emotion screams with louder voice,
On impulse I might choose to do
What reason tells me is taboo.
And so there's conflict in my heart.
I slip and stumble as I start
To walk along the path of grace,
Desiring so to see God's face.
His Spirit dwells within me, too,
To guide me toward what I should do.
Three voices whisper in my ear—
I wonder which my will will hear?

—S. W. Irlee

A gaggle of geese. A pride of lions. A murder of crows. An exaltation of larks.

It may be that the quirky richness of the English language is nowhere more evident than in expressions such as these—so-called "collective" phrases describing more than one of something. What do you call a group of toads? A *knot* of toads. How about whales? A *pod* of whales. What about pigs? A *sounder* of swine.

What, then, should we call the group of emotions that cluster together to cause us pain and turmoil as we try to deal with relationships? I propose that we call them a *commotion* of emotions. I like the sound of it, and I think that it describes the way we often feel. Much of our struggle with being single seems to revolve around the complicated interplay of different emotions and our inability to balance emotion and reason in a way that leads to godly choices. At times, we seem at the utter mercy of our feelings, each one interacting with the others and competing to influence our actions. Anger plays off jealousy, despair plays off anxiety—and the resulting confusion seems like quite a "commotion" to me.

Does the following pattern sound familiar? Two people meet. They could be of either sex—this pattern applies to same-sex friendships as well as to dating relationships between members of the opposite sex. One of the two (let's call him or her "A") develops expectations about the relationship. Depending on whether it is a friendship or a dating relationship, maybe the expectation is that the two will spend a lot of time together, or that they will be best friends. If they are of opposite genders, the expectation may be that they will become a couple, or that someday they will get married. A begins to act on that expectation. A might expect B to give their time together high priority and resents the time that B spends with other people. This situation becomes more complex if A and B are of opposite genders, and A thinks that this is a dating relationship. Then whole worlds of expectations open up that do not pertain to mere friends. A whole culture of dating comes into play that involves what each party is "supposed" to do.

At some point, B resents A's expectations because B does not share A's view of the relationship. Conflict arises. B finally shatters A's false expectations. A is hurt and resentful. A may lash out at B in some way, either saying something hurtful to B's face or saying negative things about B behind his or her back. B, hurt in turn by A's actions and feeling in the right, responds in kind. The walls of bitterness and resentment grow in both hearts. Christian fellowship is destroyed, and unity is negated. The sibling relationship that exists by virtue of their mutual relationship to Christ is still there, but it is estranged—any fruit that it might have born winds up rotting on the ground.

A full range of feelings is involved, a true "commotion of emotions": bitterness, anger, envy, hatred, and self-hate. No one likes to be rejected. Rejection strikes deep, cutting to the very root of our self-esteem and challenging our self-worth. It makes us question our value to ourselves, to each other, and even to God. These are strong emotions; we can easily let them dictate to us what we should do and how we should do it. As a result we often wind up doing a lot of wrong things in the wrong ways for the wrong reasons, hurting ourselves and each other.

"What Will You Do? What *Will* You Do?"

Think about it for a minute. How does one decide what action to take in a given situation? Some of us respond impulsively, going along with the first emotion we feel. Others analyze everything to death—sifting through all of the possible scenarios trying to find the one with the most favorable outcome. The competition between intellect and emotion to influence volition has been described in various ways. One description is that our "thinker" and our "feeler" do battle to influence our "chooser" to respond in a certain way.[1] As Christians, we have a third input to the "chooser"—input that is not active in non-Christians—the Holy Spirit. Our will is spiritually, intellectually, and emotionally informed. It is crucial for us to understand that we are different than we were before the Spirit of God came to dwell in our hearts. Now, in addition to the voices of our "thinker" and our "feeler," we can hear His voice.

We must be careful in letting the voices of intellect and emotion influence our choices. Those voices are contaminated and tainted, stained by the residue of the "old self," our "sin natures." God is in the process of renewing these, of making them Christlike, but that job is not yet complete. In the area of relationships, our intellects and emotions may also be contaminated by what the world has modeled before us—even by what our parents and families have modeled before us as examples of the way men and women treat each other. We should be wary of giving any one voice too much weight. Too often, we make decisions with a very unbalanced polling of the spiritual, intellectual, and emotional delegates in the congress of our will. Too often, we react in unthinking emotion or with unfeeling reason or on an unbiblical impulse that we think is spiritual. The result is often hurt and sorrow rather than the enrichment of our brothers and sisters. We may also damage whatever witness we might have had with those who do not know the Lord had we acted in a more balanced way. Like our own government—in which the executive, judiciary, and legislative branches exercise "checks and balances" against each other—we need to be careful not to act either emotionally without thinking or coldly and logically without feeling. And how often do we act without weighing spiritual input at all, without even praying, so that God might influence our choices through His Spirit? When we are dating, when our self-esteem is involved, or when there are expectations of romance, marriage, and sex, there is a tremendous potential for destruction when we allow our emotional turmoil to make us react impulsively.

A particular commotion of emotions crops up again and again, especially when spurned love, bruised self-esteem, or unfulfilled expectations are at issue. If we can see these emotions for what they are and learn how God tells us to deal with them according to His Word, maybe we can balance the three inputs to our choosers and make decisions that will glorify God rather than gratify ourselves. Consider the following thoughts, and vignettes from Scripture, when trying to manage the commotion of emotions.

Envy

Most of us have wanted someone to like us or love us and have tried to capture that person's attention and affection. Then it became painfully obvious that the object of our campaign preferred someone else. Many of us have had the heart-numbing experience of seeing someone we once loved marry another. How easy it is to rail against God for allowing such a thing to happen—to curse Him for not giving us what we wanted so badly. How easily we question God's love for us and wonder why, if He really loves us, He refuses to give us what we so desired. And how easy it is to resent, maybe even hate, the person who got what we wanted—"Why is he [or she] more deserving than I? Is he [or she] a better person than I?"

A story in Scripture speaks to this question—we find it at the end of the gospel of John. After His death and resurrection, Jesus appears to the disciples. John tells us that this occasion is the third time that Jesus has appeared to them since His resurrection. Peter and some of the other disciples are fishing but are having no luck. Jesus appears, standing on the beach, and asks them if they have caught anything. When they say no, He tells them to cast their nets on the starboard side of the boat. After hauling up a huge load of fish, John realizes that the man on the beach is Jesus. In typically impulsive fashion, Peter dives into the water and swims for shore.

Jesus makes breakfast for the disciples and then spends

some "quality time" with them. In particular, he focuses on Peter. They are probably walking along the shore of the Sea of Tiberias, where they have been fishing. Three times Jesus asks Peter if he loves Him. Three times Peter answers "yes"— a heart-tugging counterpoint to Peter's earlier three-fold denial of the Lord. Jesus tells Peter three times to tend His flock and be its shepherd. Jesus then tells Peter a little about his own future and what it will hold.

But Peter is distracted:

> Peter, turning around, saw the disciple whom Jesus loved following them; the one who also had leaned back on His bosom at the supper and said, "Lord, who is the one who betrays You?" So Peter seeing him said to Jesus, "Lord, and what about this man?"[2]

Picture this scene in your mind. Peter has just been spending time "one-on-one" with the risen Christ, a unique and amazing experience in itself. In what Jesus has just said, He has implied that Peter will have a significant impact on the spread of the gospel and on the growth of the church, that he will live to a ripe old age, and ultimately die a death that is glorifying to God. But Peter notices that John is following them, and he wonders what John's future would be—perhaps worrying that it might eclipse his own. Listen to what Jesus says in response:

> Jesus said to him, "If I want him to remain until I come, what is that to you? You follow Me!"[3]

Jesus tells Peter not to concern himself with John's future but to focus on obediently walking in the steps of the Lord. "You follow Me!" He says. That is the remedy for us as well when we are envious of what others have or what we think they have, when they get what we want or what we think we want. When we see friends getting married before we do, when we see someone getting all of the dates while we sit at home, when we see couples walking arm-in-arm and wonder when we will be one half of a couple, we need to focus on Jesus. We need to commit ourselves to following Him. We need to keep our eyes on Him, believing that He will meet our needs in the right way and at the right time if we only continue to follow Him. He has told us amazing truth about ourselves; He has made amazing promises to us as well as to Peter. But we need to get the focus off of anyone else—off ourselves, as well—and simply follow Him. Do what He has asked us to do. Serve. Love others. Be His witnesses. Live out His love.

There is an important caveat: He might not meet our needs in the way we desire or in the way we envision. Focusing on Jesus is not saying, "I will grit my teeth and concentrate on ministry for now, enduring until He finally gives me what I want." That approach is merely envy postponed. Focusing on Jesus, applying to ourselves His command for Peter means being willing to follow Him wherever He leads—whether that is into a lifetime of singleness or a brief season of singleness followed by marriage. We cannot go through life comparing ourselves with others—"keeping up with the Joneses"—in the dating realm or in any other realm of our lives. Envy will cripple us as effective servants—we cannot keep our eyes on Jesus if they are constantly darting over to see what our brothers and sisters are getting.

Anxiety

The insistent ticking of our biological clocks and the anxiety produced by that inexorable progression has been parodied in every medium from comic strips to television shows. But parody always contains an element of truth, and it is true that as we see ourselves getting older, with no prospect of marriage on the horizon, we begin to worry and grow anxious. As we go through long periods without dating or through one failed relationship after another, it is inevitable that we become anxious: "Will I ever find someone?" "Is God ever going to provide me with a mate? With children?" "When will I be happy?" "When will I be fulfilled?" That awful empty feeling grows inside us—the fear that God will not provide. We keep hoping that His provision is just over the horizon, just out of sight. But deep down we have a horrible fear that when we get over the horizon, we will find nothing there. What we thought was there has disappeared like a mirage in the desert. Do we really believe that God will meet our needs? Really?

What does God say about anxiety? How would God have us deal with that doubt, with the fear that He won't provide? Listen to what Jesus said:

> "For this reason I say to you, do not be worried about your life, as to what you will eat or what you will drink; nor for your body, as to what you will put on. Is not life more than food, and the body more than clothing? Look at the birds of the air, that they do not sow, nor reap nor gather into barns, and yet your heavenly Father feeds them. Are you not worth much more than they? And who of you by being worried can add a single hour to his life? And why are you worried about clothing? Observe how the lilies of the field grow; they do not toil nor do they spin, yet I say to you that not even Solomon in all his glory clothed himself like one of these. But if God so clothes the grass of the field, which is alive today and tomorrow is thrown into the furnace, will He not much more clothe you? You of little faith! Do not worry, then, saying, 'What will we eat?' or 'What will we drink?' or 'What will we wear for clothing?' For the Gentiles

eagerly seek all these things; for your heavenly Father knows that you need all these things. But seek first His kingdom and His righteousness, and all these things will be added to you. So do not worry about tomorrow; for tomorrow will care for itself. Each day has enough trouble of its own."[4]

Most of us do not have trouble trusting God for food to eat and water to drink or clothes to wear. When haven't we had these things? It is easy to trust that God will continue providing something that we have always had—especially when we live in a prosperous and comfortable society. There are people to whom we can turn for help—family, friends, the church, the government. Through some effort of our own, we can probably get what we need.

But to whom do we turn to get a spouse? What effort of our own is sufficient to get us the person we want, at the time we want, in the way we want? Given money, we can run out and buy food, drink, and clothing, but there is no "Mates-R-Us" store at which to shop for spouses. It is easy to trust God for the things we are in little danger of going without. It is easy to trust God for things we can reasonably get for ourselves. It is in trusting Him when things look hopeless or look as though they are going to take forever that we have trouble.

The principle for doing so, however, is the same as in that passage from Matthew; God knows what we need to sustain life, and He promises to provide what we need. Anxiety is unproductive: "Who of you by being worried can add a single hour to his life?" Or perhaps it could read: "Which of you by worrying can find yourself a mate?" And anxiety is unnecessary: "Your heavenly Father knows that you need all these things." Or perhaps, "Your heavenly Father knows what kind of partner you need and when you need that person."

Fine. That is a great truth. But how do we grab hold of that and live it out? How do we remove that haunting feeling deep in our hearts that God will not provide what we need? No matter how much our intellects tell us that it is true, our emotions are crying out in panic. What do we do? Jesus said to "seek first His kingdom and His righteousness, and all these things will be added to you." One of the first songs I remember learning as a Christian had this verse as its lyrics. You probably have sung it, too. How many times have you sung it and realized the context from which it is drawn? How many times have you sung it and realized that it reveals the answer to anxiety? We are to focus on God's kingdom and seek His righteousness above all else—above the satisfaction of our needs, be they for food or for a mate. He will provide what we really need, though not necessarily what we think we need or want. We are to get our eyes off ourselves and the selfish, self-indulgent consideration of our own needs and focus on Him, on ministering to others, on being His witnesses, and on edifying and strengthening His body.

However, that is not to say that we should be unaware of our needs. Many times they are legitimate, and it is appropriate to confess our needs and our wants before God. How do we do that if not through prayer? I think that we often fail to realize the crucial role of prayer in combating anxiety. In Philippians 4:6–7, Paul says,

> Be anxious for nothing, but in everything by prayer and supplication with thanksgiving let your requests be made known to God. And the peace of God, which surpasses all comprehension, will guard your hearts and your minds in Christ Jesus.

It is easy for us, in the midst of desperate desire, to pray that God will satisfy our needs. But how do we pray and for what do we pray? Do our prayers sometimes become merely a mechanical recitation of what we want God to do for us? "Please, God—I need a wife, I need a wife, I need a wife— now!" or, "Lord, I really think I'm in love with the person who doesn't know I'm alive. Change his heart, change his heart, please, change his heart!" The more times we pray it, the greater the chance that we will get what we want. Right? Jesus addressed this topic, saying,

> "And when you are praying, do not use meaning- less repetition as the Gentiles do, for they suppose that they will be heard for their many words. So do not be like them; for your Father knows what you need before you ask Him."[5]

He gives an example, the Lord's Prayer. It is a prayer that truly "seeks first His kingdom and His righteousness." That is the key element that we so often miss. It is not wrong to bring our desires and our longings before the Lord in prayer. Quite the contrary. But often we expect that He will answer them in the way we want and at the time we want. We do not "make our requests known to God" with "thanksgiv- ing"—giving thanks to Him in our hearts for hearing and responding to our prayers regardless of how He chooses to answer them. We do not recognize that He knows what we need before we ask Him. We act as though the purpose of our prayers is to inform God of our need rather than to confess that we depend utterly on Him to provide what He already knows we need.

Perhaps we need to learn to relax in God's arms. Perhaps we need to get to the point where we trust Him completely to meet our needs. Jesus, at one point in His ministry, sent His disciples out to "proclaim the kingdom of God and to perform healing." He told them,

"Take nothing for your journey, neither a staff, nor a bed, nor bread, nor money; and do not even have two tunics apiece. Whatever house you enter, stay there until you leave that city."[6]

That might not sound like good advice for the well-prepared traveler, but Jesus was trying to teach the Twelve to depend on God to provide what they needed, to live in the reality of God's power and provision. We need to learn the same lesson. We need to surrender our anxiety to the Lord and rest assured that He will provide what we need (but not necessarily what we want) at the time that we need it (but not necessarily when we would like to have it). If God in His infinite and amazing love for us is going to provide us with a mate, He will do it in His way and in His time. We have to learn to be comfortable with that and recognize that worry will not bring about His provisions any faster.

Bitterness

Most of us have probably been rejected by someone we thought we loved and whose love we sought in return, and perhaps we became bitter and angry. Rejection is the fuse, and bitterness is the powder keg that explodes and lays waste to our emotional and spiritual health as well as our ability to reach out in love to others. Other fuses also exist, and they come in different lengths. But no matter how the explosion is triggered, it has tremendous destructive potential.

The following situation crops up in a lot of different kinds of relationships—friendships, dating relationships, marriages, and even other kinds of partnerships: one party to the relationship views the relationship differently than does the other person. For example, a man and a woman have gone out together a few times. The woman views the relationship as being merely a friendship; the man thinks that it is something more. Each party places very different expectations on the other. The man, thinking that this is a serious dating relationship, expects that the woman will not see other men in a dating context. He thinks that she should be available to do things with him in order to strengthen their relationship. The woman, viewing the relationship as merely a friendship, resents the man's placing constraints on her. The situation eventually comes to a head when she finds another man whom she is interested in dating. She dumps the first man, finally making it clear to him that she has viewed their relationship all along as being "just friends." The man, his romantic hopes dashed, becomes bitter, angry, and sick at heart. In his mind, according to his expectations, the relationship was headed along the path to marriage. He resents the woman for having derailed it, for misleading him, for making him think that she was interested when she was not. His heart grows cold and resentful toward her. The powder keg of bitterness explodes in his heart, and he is no longer able to treat her as a sister in Christ and no longer able to practice Paul's injunction to "through love serve one another." Like Job, he sits and cries out, wondering why God, who supposedly loves him, lets something like this happen.

> "I loathe my own life; I will give full vent to my complaint; I will speak in the bitterness of my soul. I will say to God, 'Do not condemn me; let me know why You contend with me.'"[7]

How does one deal with these emotions? Is there a way to defuse the powder keg of bitterness before it explodes and destroys? Yes. Paul tells us in Ephesians,

> Let all bitterness and wrath and anger and clamor and
> slander be put away from you, along with all malice.[8]

Fine. But how does one do that? As with so many other aspects of our lives as Christians, I think that the answer is so obvious and so easy that we miss it—or more usually, we are simply not willing to act accordingly. The "putting away" of these things is part and parcel of who we are in Christ, but too often we refuse to accept that fact, preferring instead to harbor and nurture the bitterness. After all, nursing a grudge gives a certain perverse satisfaction. It can feel satisfying to resent someone, to plot revenge against enemies, to figure out how to hurt those who have hurt you.

That sounds pretty awful, doesn't it? It should. Embracing hate, revenge, and hurtfulness is characteristic of the life from which Jesus died to redeem us and to bring us out. Earlier in that same passage in Ephesians, Paul talks about it:

> So this I say, and affirm together with the Lord, that
> you walk no longer just as the Gentiles also walk, in
> the futility of their mind, being darkened in their
> understanding, excluded from the life of God because
> of the ignorance that is in them, because of the
> hardness of their heart and they, having become
> callous, have given themselves over to sensuality
> for the practice of every kind of impurity with
> greediness.[9]

That seems to include harboring bitterness in one's heart, holding a grudge, and plotting revenge, wouldn't you say? Paul continues:

> But you did not learn Christ in this way, if indeed
> you have heard Him and have been taught in Him,
> just as truth is in Jesus, that, in reference to your

former manner of life, you lay aside the old self, which is being corrupted in accordance with the lusts of deceit, and that you be renewed in the spirit of your mind, and put on the new self, which in the likeness of God has been created in righteousness and holiness of the truth.[10]

That's it. It is that simple. We choose to live according to our new identities; to act as those who we, in fact, are; to live as citizens of the kingdom to which Christ's death has purchased entrance. We choose. We choose to put off the old self and put on the new. We choose to allow our minds to be renewed, to look at things from God's perspective. We choose to live in the way that Christ has made possible—in righteousness and in the holiness of truth.

Paul gives several examples, which are relevant in the context of dealing with bitterness and the other hateful emotions that can be aroused when relationships go awry or expectations are not met. What does he say?

Therefore, laying aside falsehood, speak truth each one of you with his neighbor, for we are members of one another. Be angry, and yet do not sin; do not let the sun go down on your anger, and do not give the devil an opportunity. . . . Let no unwholesome word proceed from your mouth, but only such a word as is good for edification according to the need of the moment, so that it will give grace to those who hear. Do not grieve the Holy Spirit of God, by whom you were sealed for the day of redemption. . . . Be kind to one another, tender-hearted, forgiving each other, just as God in Christ also has forgiven you.[11]

So what do we do with this commotion of emotions? How do we respond to it? How do we react when our hearts are burdened by envy, anxiety, or bitterness? A common thread runs through the Scriptures we have just considered. Did you catch it? How are we to respond to envy? Jesus tells us, "You follow Me." How do we respond to anxiety? Jesus tells us to seek the Father, and Paul tells us to pray. How do we respond to bitterness? Paul tells us to put bitterness aside. These are all verbs, that is, action words, and not adjectives; they are things that we are to do, not characteristics that we are to have. I do not think that Paul's use of action words is an accident. We need to take the focus off of ourselves—off of how we might have been hurt—and put it onto others, on how we may help to heal them. We do that by serving. We do that by reaching out to each other as Christ Himself would. We do that by learning to care more about the needs of others than we care about our own needs, by stepping out to meet their needs rather than sitting back and insisting that our needs be met.

We need to surrender the expectation that others exist to meet our needs. How often that expectation cripples relationships, whether it is the fellowship of many believers in a Bible study or of two people in a marriage! Have you ever seen someone come into a fellowship clearly broadcasting the message "I am needy—love me"? Such individuals often enter a group with some preexisting disgruntlement—some envy, some anxiety, some bitterness from past events. They stay in the group long enough to see whether or not they will be on the receiving end of love. But if they do not receive the treatment they expect, they may well become more disgruntled, more envious, more anxious, and more bitter. Anger grows and resentment festers. Whether we are one-in-twenty in a Bible study or one-in-two in a marriage, we cannot let hurt arise from the failures of other persons to meet our expectations. God promises to meet our needs; there is no promise that any other individual will do so.

From an eternal perspective, whether we fall in love or

whether we marry is probably of little import—except as it contributes to the process of renewal that God is performing in each of us and as it gives us the opportunity to participate in the renewal process of our spouses. It is our eternal relationship with Him that is crucial. We are bound together as brothers and sisters in our common relationship to Jesus. That is an eternal relationship, too. How sad that in focusing on the temporary we may sour the eternal by letting our hurt feelings get in the way. How sad that we choose to sacrifice fellowship and the joy of seeing each other mature in the Lord because of unfulfilled romantic expectations and desires. Can't we put those aside? Can't we work through the disappointment and the disillusionment together, "speaking the truth in love"?

It is not easy to walk in obedience to Christ. It is not easy to yield our intellects and emotions and wills to the control of the Holy Spirit. It is not easy, but it is essential. The process of learning to make that choice is much of what our growing up as His children is all about. As we choose Him, He changes us. Sometimes it seems impossible. Sometimes it seems futile. Sometimes it seems confusing. But it should never seem hopeless. His power and promise are sufficient to make it happen.

Consider This

1. What destructive emotions do you most often confront in your life as a single Christian?
2. Are your decisions most often governed more by your emotions or by your reason? How might you move toward a more balanced decision-making process?
3. What practical things might you do to serve others and take your focus off yourself?

chapter eight

The Swirling Vortex of Desire

I struggled briefly to free myself from the steel vise of his arms, but it was only a token resistance. . . . Dean's lips descended swiftly . . . and I knew why I had consented to meet him. . . . The kiss was like a drug which seized control of my brain . . . and enveloped me in a warm cloud of rapture. . . . I was a weightless thing that rose through the air without effort, to soar over vast distances!! Dean's voice filtered through the joy-giving mists . . . "I knew it, baby! You could never leave Uncle Dean!" From Dean's vain smile of triumph, I learned the gravity of my predicament! I had only a few seconds left to reassert myself before I forfeited Bill Walker's genuine love and became a hopeless addict to Dean Leonard's deceiving arms!!! (From *Back Door Love*, a 1950s romance comic.)

When it comes to physical attraction, it is often very difficult to act with a balanced consensus of intellect, emotion, and spirit. How often do people regret doing something "in the passion of the moment"? How often do we embark on a romance knowing only that a person is physically attractive? How often do we run ahead of God's intention by indulging too quickly in the physical pleasures that He designed to be enjoyed only in the context of marriage?

Emotions are powerful. Physical attraction—what we often call chemistry—is powerful. But too often we let ourselves get caught up in what a friend of mine calls "the swirling vortex of desire." We enjoy the rush of spinning in that whirlpool, oblivious to the dangers and to the damage that it causes to our relationships with others and with God.

Vortices pull us down into their depths—into the depths of a committed relationship when we experience passion in the way that God intended, or into the depths of destructive behavior, despair, and regret when we abuse it. To avoid being overwhelmed by the vortex, we need to listen not only to our emotions but also to our intellect and to what God is telling us through His Holy Spirit as we read and meditate upon His Word. However, it often seems that our emotions shout at us whereas our intellect protests in a nervous stammer, and the Spirit whispers so gently that we ignore His counsel.

Single Christians struggle with two particular areas related to the swirling vortex of desire. The first area concerns how much weight we should give to physical attractiveness in evaluating the potential of a new relationship. This area of concern overlaps with the broader question of what we look for (or should look for) in a mate (see chap. 2). The second area concerns the difficulty of maintaining sexual purity while caught in the grip of the vortex.

Better Living Through Chemistry

There is nothing wrong with physical attraction—sometimes described as "chemistry" or as a "spark"—toward a member of the opposite sex. God gave us bodies that are capable of perceiving and responding to physical attractiveness. This was His intention when He created the first man and the first woman. As seen in chapter 1, Adam invested much time and energy in naming the animals, finally coming to the realization that there was none like him. So what did he say upon being presented with the mate whom God had designed especially for him? The first word he uttered was an enthusiastic *"This!"* As it is recorded in the Hebrew text of Genesis, the scene is quite dramatic. The word *this* in Hebrew is pronounced like "zoath" (rhyming with "oath"). I imagine Adam giving it a throaty utterance, a guttural vocalization mingling astonishment, wonder, passion, relief, and gratitude. Our English translations somewhat obscure Adam's enthusiasm—his exclamation is repeated three times in the Hebrew text, so that what he actually said was something like *"This* now at last is bone from my bones and flesh from my flesh, *this* shall be called woman because from man was taken *this!"*

God's good intention in building chemistry into the relationship between a man and a woman is described immediately following the introduction of Eve to Adam. That attraction was to provide the impetus for maturing humans to "leave and cleave"—to leave the protection and security of their parents and cleave to their mates in the creation of a new entity through marriage. In some places in Scripture, we detect the swirl of the vortex, and marriage follows from it. It seems to have been at work when Jacob chose Rachel, whose "form and face" were beautiful, over Leah, whose "weak eyes" apparently lacked a vivacious sparkle. It may have been there when Boaz first noticed Ruth. Solomon and the Shulammite explicitly and unashamedly express in Song of Solomon the attraction that they feel for each other. But we could also think of instances where acting on the impulse of attraction without thought or prayer was a devastating mistake—for example, when David gazed upon

Bathsheba and when Samson beheld Delilah. The strength and essential nature of the attraction may have been the same in all of these cases, but the circumstances, context, and outcome were vastly different.

Is it wise to become romantically involved with someone just because they have been packaged attractively? Is it wrong to do so? What role does chemistry play in a relationship, and how should we factor it into our thinking? The viewpoint of the Christian community spans both extremes: some Christians say that you should find someone to whom you are strongly attracted and pray that God will work out the details; others say that you should find someone who is well-grounded spiritually and learn to love their looks. Should we pursue someone for whom we feel an immediate and intense attraction, even if that person is not spiritually compatible? Should we seek someone whose character inspires a lifetime commitment, even if that person is not the most attractive person we have ever met?

Particularly when we are young (chronologically and spiritually), we too often err on the side of letting physical attraction sway us, leading us too readily into relationships that are spiritually incompatible. Surely God meant marriage to be sustained by more than physical attraction, no matter how strong. On the other hand, some Christian marriages are built simply on commitment, without benefit of that "spark." Martin Luther said of his fiancée, "I am not madly in love, but I cherish her."[1] But surely God meant marriage to be sustained by more than dogged determination, no matter how pious or well-intentioned.

As with so many other aspects of our lives as Christians, perhaps a reasoned balance is the key. Look at God's relationship to Israel, which is portrayed throughout Scripture in terms of a marriage. In English, our "love vocabulary" is somewhat impoverished, so in order to communicate about this subject we sometimes resort to such adolescent idioms as "Do you just like him, or do you '*like* him' like him?" Fortunately, Hebrew is more expressive. Two terms are used in the Old Testament to picture the love relationship. One is *'ahabah;* the other is *chesed.* J. I. Packer describes the difference:

> God's *'ahabah* [is] from the verb *'aheb,* meaning "love"—election love, as Dr. Snaith calls it. . . . This is the love whereby God chose Israel to be his people—spontaneous, selective, unconditional, unevoked, undeserved love. . . . The other term involved is God's *chesed . . .* the basic thought behind the word is of God's resolute loyalty to the people to whom he has pledged himself. Snaith calls it his covenant-love; it is essentially a matter of faithfulness to the covenant promise whereby he bound himself to be Israel's God and to use all of the resources of deity to bless them.[2]

The enduring relationship of marriage involves both kinds of love. Any relationship that develops beyond casual friendship necessarily involves an element of choosing, an element that is "spontaneous, selective, unconditional, unevoked, undeserved." This is true not only in romantic relationships but also in deeper friendships. But sustaining a marriage for a lifetime requires a kind of loyal-love that is persistent, that does not wax or wane in response to circumstances, a love that arises from "faithfulness to the covenant promise"—in this case the pledge to love "from this day forward, for better or for worse, for richer or for poorer, in sickness and in health, till death do us part."

"Sanct" Singleness

Single Christians often speak of wanting to know the "will of God" for their love lives. By this, they usually mean that they want answers to specific questions: "Should I go out with this person?" "Is this the person God wants me to marry?"

We ought, then, to pay particular attention to Scripture that explicitly teaches us what the will of God is. In fact, only two such places exist in the New Testament: 1 Peter 2:15 and 1 Thessalonians 4:1–8. The latter reference is relevant to our discussion, and there Paul writes,

> Finally then, brethren, we request and exhort you in the Lord Jesus, that as you received from us instruction as to how you ought to walk and please God (just as you actually do walk), that you excel still more. For you know what commandments we gave you by the authority of the Lord Jesus. For this is the will of God, your sanctification; that is, that you abstain from sexual immorality; that each of you know how to possess his own vessel in sanctification and honor, not in lustful passion, like the Gentiles who do not know God; and that no man transgress and defraud his brother in the matter because the Lord is the avenger in all these things, just as we also told you before and solemnly warned you. For God has not called us for the purpose of impurity, but in sanctification. So, he who rejects this is not rejecting man but the God who gives His Holy Spirit to you.

Here, Paul specifically identifies the will of God: our sanctification. What does he mean by *sanctification?* In both Old Testament Hebrew and New Testament Greek, a single word-group is used to express the ideas conveyed by our two English words *sanctification* and *holiness*. J. I. Packer has wryly observed that our appreciation of the intimate relationship between these two words might be strengthened if English contained the adjective *sanct* and the verb *holify*. But it does not; therefore, we are stuck with using two different English words to convey what Hebrew and Greek do with one word.[3] That is, rather than saying that "to sanctify" means to make something "sanct," or that "to holify" means to make something "holy," we wind up saying that "to sanctify" something means to make it "holy."

In the original languages, the idea of sanctifying something involves setting it apart and separating it from that which is not holy. Warren Wiersbe illustrates this well:

> The Sabbath was holy because God set it apart for His people (Exod. 16:23). The priests were holy because they were set apart to minister to the Lord (Lev. 21:7–8). Their garments were holy and could not be duplicated for common use (Exod. 28:2). The tithe that the people brought was holy (Lev. 27:30). Anything that God said was holy had to be treated differently from the common things of life in the Hebrew camp. In fact, the camp of Israel was holy, because the Lord dwelt there with His people (Deut. 23:14).[4]

The architecture of Israel's temple (and even earlier, the tabernacle) helps further illustrate this idea. The temple was divided into regions with progressively increasing holiness and progressively restricted access. In the temple as it existed in Jesus' and Paul's time there was an outer court that anyone, even Gentiles, could enter as long as they behaved with appropriate decorum and reverence. Ascending a few steps from this court, one encountered another court that only Jews could enter. A wall barred the way between the two courts, and upon this wall was inscribed the penalty attached to violating this prohibition:

> No foreigner is to enter within the balustrade and enclosure around the temple area. Whoever is caught will have himself to blame for his death which will follow.[5]

Beyond and above this area was another court that only the men of Israel could enter. Within this court was an area that only the priests could enter. Inside this area was the sanctuary, which contained the Holy Place, and beyond that, in the innermost part of the temple, the Holiest Place or the Holy of Holies. The Holy Place contained the seven-branched golden lampstand, the table of showbread, and the altar of incense, which were used by the priests throughout the year in performing various ceremonies. Access to the Holiest Place, however, was much more restrictive; it could be entered only by the High Priest and even then only on one day of the year—the Day of Atonement. Thus, from the multitude of peoples daily thronging the Court of the Gentiles, access to the most intimate experience of God's presence was ultimately narrowed to only one person on only one day.[6]

The architecture of the temple was designed to provide a tangible, visible reminder of a crucial theological truth— that there is a gulf between man in his fallen state and God in His perfect righteousness that necessitates a separation between the two. Sanctification is all about God's bringing us into His presence, making us acceptable to stand before Him, separating us from the realm of the profane, and bringing us into the realm of the holy, bridging that gulf by conferring something of His righteousness upon us.

In 1 Thessalonians 4, Paul lists three specific actions that reflect our sanctification, three choices we can make that move us away from operating in the realm of what is unholy toward operating in the realm of what is holy. These three items are all related to our sexual behavior:

1. "that you abstain from sexual immorality";
2. "that each of you know how to possess his own vessel in sanctification and honor, not in lustful passion, like the Gentiles who do not know God"; and
3. "that no man transgress and defraud his brother in the matter."

Let's look at these items individually.

"That you abstain from sexual immorality."

To many in modern society, abstinence is a repulsive, antiquated concept, a relic of the repressed Victorian era, as is the idea that anything sexual could or should be thought "immoral." The suggestion that one might voluntarily deny oneself something pleasurable is thought to be the height of absurdity. But our age is not unique in this viewpoint; something of the same could be said of Paul's world. Popular opinion assigned no stigma to sex outside of marriage. F. F. Bruce remarks,

> Christianity from the outset has sanctified sexual union with marriage (as in Judaism); outside marriage it was forbidden. This was a strange notion in the pagan society to which the gospel was first brought; there various forms of extramarital sexual union were tolerated and some were even encouraged. A man might have a mistress . . . who could provide him also with intellectual companionship; the institution of slavery made it easy for him to have a concubine . . . while casual gratification was

readily available from a harlot. . . . The function of his wife was to manage his household and be the mother of his legitimate children and heirs. There was no body of public opinion to discourage [sexual immorality], although someone who indulged in it to excess might be satirized on the same level as a notorious glutton or drunkard. Certain forms of religion, indeed, involved ritual [sexual immorality].[7]

In the insistence of Christianity—and of Judaism before it—that sexual relations be confined to marriage, we see an example of God's creating a boundary, much like the one separating the Court of the Gentiles from the rest of the temple. God scribes this dividing line and says, "This boundary separates those who know Me from those who do not. My people operate within this boundary and do not step across it; those who do not know me operate outside it." As we have said, the presence of such a division is part of what sanctification is all about: the separation of that which is holy from that which is unholy.

Scripture repeatedly defines boundaries related to sexual purity that God's people may not cross. In the Old Testament, for example, Leviticus 20 identifies several sexual relationships that are forbidden to the people of God, because "you shall consecrate yourselves therefore and be holy, for I am the LORD your God. You shall keep My statutes and practice them; I am the LORD who sanctifies you" (vv. 7–8). In the New Testament, Paul, in particular, emphasizes this point:

The body is not for immorality, but for the Lord.[8]

Flee immorality. Every other sin that a man commits is outside the body, but the immoral man sins against his own body. Or do you not know that your body is a temple of the Holy Spirit who is in you, whom you have from God, and that you are not your own? For you have been bought with a price: therefore glorify God in your body.[9]

I am afraid that when I come again my God may humiliate me before you, and I may mourn over many of those who have sinned in the past and not repented of the impurity, immorality and sensuality which they have practiced.[10]

But immorality or any impurity or greed must not even be named among you, as is proper among saints. . . . For this you know with certainty, that no immoral or impure person or covetous man, who is an idolater, has an inheritance in the kingdom of Christ and God.[11]

Therefore consider the members of your earthly body as dead to immorality, impurity, passion, evil desire, and greed.[12]

If we wish to know the will of God for our lives as single Christians, why not start here with what is stated explicitly? If we desire to live in a manner that honors God and brings Him glory, we are actively to keep away from sexual immorality—indeed, in the second of the preceding passages, we are told not merely to avoid it but to run away from it!

When we fail to obey this injunction, we bring the profane into the presence of the holy. We have seen how the architecture of Israel's temple complex defined increasingly holy spaces. Within this building was the Holy Place, which, in addition to the lampstand, incense altar, and showbread table mentioned earlier, contained other articles used in worship—bowls, cups, spoons, tongs, and censers made of pure gold.[13]

Beyond that was the Holiest Place (or the Holy of Holies), into which God's divine presence condescended to enter.

About two centuries before the time of Jesus, Israel came under the rule of a brutal Syrian tyrant named Antiochus Epiphanes.[14] In retaliation for the jubilation shown by the Israelites over a false report of his death in battle during a campaign in Egypt, Antiochus sacked the temple, stealing many of the sacred objects and sacrificing an unclean animal—a pig—on the altar of the temple. The Jews were horrified and desolated:

> Rulers and elders groaned;
> girls and young men wasted away;
> the women's beauty suffered a change;
> every bridegroom took up a dirge,
> the bride sat grief-stricken on her marriage bed.
> The very land quaked for its inhabitants
> and the whole House of Jacob was clothed with
>   shame.[15]

Paul identifies our bodies as being temples of the Holy Spirit. Just as God's presence resided in the Holy of Holies, He now resides in us through the indwelling of His Spirit. Thus, our involvement in sexual immorality is no less a desecration than Antiochus Epiphanes's looting and irreverent sacrifice. It brings the profane into the presence of the holy in exactly same way. That image is strong and disturbing, but it might do us good to reflect upon it as we are tempted toward immoral choices.

"That each of you know how to possess his own vessel in sanctification and honor, not in lustful passion, like the Gentiles who do not know God."

We who know God are to act in a way that distinguishes

us from those who do not. But what does Paul mean when he speaks of "possessing" one's own "vessel"? Usually, the Greek word *skeuos,* which is translated here as "vessel," means just that—a container. For example, Leviticus 11:33 describes how an inanimate object—such as a clay pot—can become unfit for use by coming into contact with unclean animals. The rendition of the Leviticus verse in the Greek Septuagint uses the word *skeuos* for the clay pot.

However, Paul is not speaking about literal clay pots, but instead is using a metaphor. If we are familiar with Paul's other writings, we might recall phrases such as "we have this treasure in earthen vessels, so that the surpassing greatness of the power will be of God and not from ourselves,"[16] or "Therefore, if anyone cleanses himself from these things, he will be a vessel for honor, sanctified, useful to the Master, prepared for every good work."[17] From these examples we might conclude that Paul is using *vessel* figuratively to describe our bodies or our "selves." In the context of this passage, then, he would be speaking of our bodies in their sexual capabilities or as instruments of sexual expression. Indeed, some commentators argue that Paul is using *skeuos* as a euphemism for our sexual organs themselves. This usage is seen in nonbiblical Greek, and it also occurs in the Septuagint.[18]

The word translated "possess" can have the sense of "mastering," or "gaining control over." So whether Paul had in mind the body in its sexual function or specifically the sexual organs, he is communicating is the same idea: "gain mastery over your sexual desires and behaviors."

Is this not, then, a standard by which we can evaluate our decisions and behaviors? Allowing ourselves to get into situations where we are vulnerable (such as being alone with a member of the opposite sex in the dark late at night) is not conducive to exercising mastery over our sexual natures. Making excuses such as "I was swept away by the passion of the moment" or "I just couldn't help myself" does not reflect self-control, either.

It hardly needs to be said (but I will, anyway): Our culture does not give us much support in attaining of mastery over our sexual desires and behaviors. Although the cries of those who champion sexual freedom and experimentation are perhaps less shrill than they were thirty years ago during the heyday of the "Sexual Revolution," that is only because the message they voiced has largely been accepted. The strident shouts of the past have simply been replaced by a pervasive, persistent murmuring that affirms sexual self-indulgence as a fundamental right.

The explicitness of sexuality in our culture has increased steadily during my lifetime. In the early 1960s, it was still considered taboo for television to show a married couple in the same bed. Today, virtually every prime-time television comedy or drama includes some degree of sexual activity or innuendo. Viewing pornography was once accompanied by at least some level of self-consciousness and shame and was undertaken with a certain degree of stealth. Now most people with an e-mail address are routinely bombarded with unsolicited offers of easy access to web sites that display the most explicit material imaginable.

In such a culture, is it any wonder that many biblical ideas are thought to be quaint and outdated, archaic, and obsolete? That we are not free to do with our bodies as we wish, that we ought to exercise restraint in our sexual gratification, that the intensity or immediacy of our personal sexual satisfaction is not the purest measure of what is good, that we are answerable to a higher authority than our own self-interest and lust—these principles are seen by modern culture as archaic and obsolete. Yet these principles are the ones that Scripture teaches, and if we are to honor God in our sex lives it is to those principles that we must adhere, even in the face of a flagrantly disagreeing culture.

"That no man transgress and defraud his brother in the matter."

The word translated as "transgress" has the sense of crossing a line, of overstepping a boundary, of illicitly pursuing that which is forbidden.[19] That sense fits well with the illustration explored earlier—lines of demarcation such as the one separating the Court of the Gentiles from the rest of the temple precincts. The word translated as "defraud" has the sense of seeking more than is rightfully yours and of taking advantage of someone else to obtain it.[20] Although Paul describes the object of these actions as one's "brother," it likely means "a fellow believer" of either gender.

How do we overstep boundaries and take advantage of others to obtain that to which we are not entitled in the sexual arena? Clearly, we do both when we enjoy the sexual intimacy that God intended to be reserved for marriage before we are actually married. But don't we also do it in other ways? Don't we do it when dating more than one person at the same time while being deceptive with the parties involved? Don't we do it when we entice another person to go too far, too soon in physical intimacy? Don't we do it when we profess to "not let the physical lead" in our relationships but then do just that? Don't we do it when we tell others that we are not involved in a particular ministry merely because we are seeking a relationship, when that actually is our reason for being there?

Our choices regarding sexual behavior affect not only ourselves and our own relationship to God but also those with whom we become romantically involved and their relationship to God. And when we are part of a close community of single Christians, actions that "transgress and defraud" our brothers and sisters can affect the quality of fellowship and transparency in the group as a whole. Many a once-intimate fellowship of single Christians has been poisoned by absorbing the aftermath of a broken dating relationship, especially when one or both of the parties feels deceived or defrauded.

Never Too Late

Our society glamorizes pre- and extramarital sex and questions the value of abstinence and sexual self-control. As a consequence, many men and women experience sexual intimacy before they have come to accept Christ and before they have received biblical teaching about God's design for our sexuality. And many people who have accepted Christ at an early age and have been well taught succumb before marriage to the power of their sexual desires.

Therefore, it is good to remember that "if anyone is in Christ, he is a new creature; the old things passed away; behold, new things have come."[21] We all come to God in a profane state, whether we come as virgins or as jades, but He can make us utterly new and holy. We all come to Him as common, soiled vessels. He makes us like the vessels of gold used in the Holy Place of His temple. Jesus criticized the hypocrisy of the Pharisees saying, "You clean the outside of the cup and of the dish, but inside they are full of robbery and self-indulgence . . . first clean the inside of the cup and of the dish, so that the outside of it may become clean also."[22] No matter how much we may have fallen short of God's will in the area of sexuality, God has cleansed us on the inside, an area that we can't clean up ourselves. As John tells us, "The blood of Jesus His Son cleanses us from all sin."[23]

This chapter opened with a quotation from *Back Door Love,* a comic book printed nearly half a century ago. The woman's monologue seems silly to modern ears. The somewhat comical phrase "the swirling vortex of desire" has been used to describe the feelings of attraction that well up within us and draw us toward certain members of the opposite sex. And there is indeed a lightheartedness and a giddiness about falling in love that is part of the appeal of the process, part of what has made it the topic of epic literature, lyrical music, and memorable cinema.

Some people may say, "Why not just enjoy that giddiness? Life is short. Youth is fleeting. Desire fades. Why not go with the impulse of the moment and not clutter up life with regrets? What's wrong with enjoying a passionate, romantic kiss without guilt, without analysis, without theological debate?"

God knows all about "the swirling vortex of desire." He designed it. He made it possible for us to experience it. He intended for us to enjoy it—when we do so within the boundaries that He has prescribed. But He also takes our sexuality very seriously. When we misuse the sexual powers He has given us, we also butcher pigs on holy altars. It is a flagrant affront to Him, a desecration of what He desires to be holy. He desires to make us clean, to make us holy, to enable us to be in His presence—yet He invites us not merely to submit passively to this process but to become active participants by choosing to control our passions and act honorably toward one another. Our choices contribute to our sanctification and our sanctification shapes our choices. What dignity God confers on man! He not only makes our sanctification possible but also lets us participate in the process.

Consider This

1. How far can we go physically before we become disobedient to God's intention for our sexuality? Some Christians say that a couple should not even kiss before they are engaged; others say that almost anything short of intercourse is acceptable. What do you think and why?

2. We discussed Paul's instruction to gain mastery over our sexual desires and behaviors in the context of physical interaction between an unmarried man and woman. How do you think such mastery might also apply to watching sexual scenes in movies? To viewing pornography? To masturbation?

3. Can you think of other examples of how we might transgress against and defraud each other in dating, particularly with regard to physical involvement?

chapter nine

Solitary Refinement

For solitude sometimes is best society,
And short retirement urges sweet return.
—John Milton, *Paradise Lost*

Solitude vivifies; isolation kills.
—Joseph Roux,
Meditations of a Parish Priest

When we have been unmarried just a little longer than we would like to be, singleness can seem like a journey through a trackless wasteland, a barren desert that we hope to cross quickly and escape from unscathed.

And yet, I don't know many married people (especially those with children) who do not sometimes say, "Boy, life was so much easier when we were single! No responsibilities, no commitments, no need to find a baby-sitter! We had time (not to mention energy!) to read, go to the movies, or pick up and head for the beach on the spur of the moment."

So maybe singleness really is like a desert—but one that contains not only vast stretches of dry, hot wasteland but also lush, inviting oases. When we are single, the tendency is to miss the oases and see only the sand. Once we get married, all one can recall is the cool spring hidden by shady palms; the desiccating heat and the ocean of sand are quickly forgotten.

Getting married folk to recall the deprivations of the desert in addition to its delights is the subject for a different book. In the present work, let us map out the oases and see where singleness offers opportunity for refreshment and revitalization.

Desert Bloom

The search for oases in the desert begins by considering some of our fellow believers who sought out the literal wasteland and lived there under conditions that most of us would find intolerable. They were willing to endure these deprivations because they believed that they received far more than they gave up. So if singleness is some kind of desert, maybe we have something to learn from their experiences.

In Egypt, about two hundred years after the time of Christ, people in large numbers became seized by the impulse to live alone in the wilderness in the hope of experiencing God more fully. Perhaps this impulse is not so surprising. Moses met God in the wilderness. God sojourned with the children of Israel there. David's character was molded there. John the Baptist preached there. Jesus was baptized there, overcame Satan's temptations there, and often went there to pray. So perhaps it is not surprising that pious folk, seeking to draw closer to God, thought that fleeing to the wilderness would help them do so.

The desert was also a place of testing, a crucible in which a man's heart could be tried and judged pure gold or dross. It was, as Lacarrière says, "the setting for a supreme experiment, a trial inevitably leading man out of himself, toward the Angel or the Beast, the Devil or God."[1] Maybe these men in Egypt went into the desert to find out what they were made of, to learn whether or not the faith they professed was genuine and offered any real power.

The desert was free of the distractions of life in the big city. A person's concerns were reduced to the bare essentials: food, water, and shelter. Life there had no relationships to work through, no shop to keep open or business to run, and no clutter. Life there must have powerfully concentrated one's thoughts and helped one ponder the question of what is really important in life.

Perhaps the wilderness is worth recalling when we think of our singleness. If we think that singleness is a desert in some respects—harsh, unpleasant, lonely—perhaps it also offers us the advantages that it offered our Egyptian brethren: an opportunity to draw closer to God, to test the mettle of our faith, to enjoy a measure of freedom from distraction as we think about what is important in life.

Monk-y Business

Consider the story of two men who hied into the deserts to devote themselves more fully to God. Both men were Egyptians, born in Egypt, which was then a Roman province. Both men came from reasonably well-off families. The parents of one, Anthony, were Christians; the parents of the other, Pachomius, were pagans.

Anthony was born about A.D. 251. His quest for closeness to God was triggered as a young man of about twenty when he heard the words of Jesus read in a church. He was specifically moved by the words that Christ spoke to the rich young ruler: "If you want to be perfect, go, sell your possessions, and give to the poor, and you will have treasure in heaven. Then come, follow me." Anthony did just that. He gave away the inheritance that he had received from his parents upon their death a few months before, left his younger sister in the care of a convent, and sought out an old hermit who was known as a model of self-denial and patient discipline.

Pachomius was born about fifteen years after Anthony left for the desert. When he was about twenty, Pachomius was drafted into the Roman army and stationed at a town called Antinoe. While serving there, he first heard of people called "Christians" and was drawn to them because of their kindness and generosity. He soon trusted in Jesus and became one of them. After his discharge from the army a few years later, he traveled and one day came upon a nearly deserted village. While praying at a nearby temple, he heard God speak to him, instructing him to stay and minister in that village. Eventually, he also heard of a hermit living in the desert nearby and sought him out, asking to be trained by him.

Initially, both young men sought to draw closer to God by withdrawing from the world in order to focus on Him. They both sought as mentors men who were hermits and practiced a very strict ascetic lifestyle, surviving on bread, salt, and water and on only two or three hours of sleep a night. But eventually their stories diverge. Anthony continued to pursue the life of an "anchorite" (from a Greek word meaning "to withdraw"). He lived by himself for some twenty years—first in an empty tomb and later in an abandoned Roman fort—and pursued God in solitary devotion. Pachomius, on the other hand, recognized the need for fellowship and established a community of like-minded individuals who could encourage and support each other in their quest for sanctification. He started the "cenobitic"(from the Latin word for "community") movement and is credited with building the first monastery in Christian history. From his belief in the value of community began monasticism as we think of it—groups of like-minded people who have chosen a life of particular devotion to God and have withdrawn from the world to practice it.

Undistracted Devotion or
Undevoted Distraction?

As far as we know, neither Anthony nor Pachomius ever married. Abstaining from marriage and remaining celibate have long been part and parcel of the monastic lifestyle. The reason can be traced back to the words of the apostle Paul in 1 Corinthians 7. Although modern Christians do not forego marriage as do some monastic orders—nor do we elevate celibacy as an essential condition for maximum intimacy with God—it behooves us to ponder Paul's statement for relevancy to single Christians.

In this passage, Paul says that it is better for unmarried believers to stay single. He is careful to explain that there is nothing wrong with marriage but that the ability to remain single is even better. The reason?

> I want you to be free from concern. One who is unmarried is concerned about the things of the Lord, how he may please the Lord; but one who is married is concerned about the things of the world, how he may please his wife, and his interests are divided. The woman who is unmarried, and the virgin, is concerned about the things of the Lord, that she may be holy both in body and spirit; but one who is married is concerned about the things of the world, how she may please her husband. This I say for your own benefit; not to put a restraint upon you, but to promote what is appropriate and to secure undistracted devotion to the Lord.[2]

Paul recognizes what every unmarried person suspects and every married person will readily admit. Although marriage offers many benefits and joys, it also requires even more unavoidable demands and responsibilities. Obligation to another person constrains us to be less self-centered and more self-sacrificing as we allocate our time, attention, money, thoughts, and energy. The following comments by Susan Foh are apropos:

> The married man or woman has the God-given responsibility to please his or her spouse—not to gratify foolish desires but to do what is best for the other, and that responsibility takes time and effort. The single person does not have this concern. The single woman does not have to cook for husband and children; she does not have to take his suit to be altered. The single man does not have to paint the bedroom or take his children to the dentist. The single person can and should spend more time in the Lord's service—leading or attending Bible studies, staying late after work to talk to that fellow-worker with a problem.[3]

It is not fair to say that "undistracted devotion" automatically arises from being single, or that being married inevitably condemns one to "undevoted distraction." It is true, however, that our single years can afford us greater freedom and flexibility to concentrate intently on studying God's Word, to spend unhurried time with Him in prayer, and simply to ponder the wonders of His glory and appreciate our relationship with Him.

For example, when I first began this book, nearly ten years ago, I was still single. That's why I began it—to seek answers for some of the questions that my singleness raised. Back then, it was easy to stay up half the night, poring over reference books and typing thoughts into my computer. Now, as I finish preparing the book for publication, as a man married six years with one small child and another one on the way, I can affirm that finding time is much more difficult than it once was! Generally, being available for ministry was much easier and more spon-taneous when I was single. Having children to raise puts greater constraints on my and my wife's time than we had when we were first married. Being married is wonderful, but being realistic requires admitting that Paul is right—being single gives one the ability to focus on serving God with fewer distractions and greater flexibility.

Scholars and theologians have debated for centuries regarding the merits or defects of lifelong singleness, whether there is such a thing as a "gift of celibacy," and so forth. But we don't know *a priori* if we will wind up married, if we will spend our whole lives pining for marriage, or if we will eventually decide that God's call to serve Him requires us to remain single. Jesus implies that the latter calling is extended to some individuals. He speaks of those who have "made themselves eunuchs for the sake of the kingdom of heaven,"[4] that is, who have chosen to abstain from sexual relations and marriage and to concentrate on serving God. (Jesus meant this figuratively; however, Origen, the third-century theologian, took His words literally and castrated himself in a fit of enthusiasm for compliance with this verse. He later recanted his literal interpretation, dramatically illustrating the importance of careful exegesis and thoughtful hermeneutics!)

The history of the church abounds with those who have foregone marriage to focus on ministry, Jesus Himself being the most obvious and notable example. Although it is possible that Paul was married at one time,[5] it seems clear that he was single during his ministry.[6] A good modern example is preacher, teacher, and theologian John R. W. Stott, who has said,

> In spite of rumors to the contrary, I have never taken
> a solemn vow or heroic decision to remain single!
> On the contrary, during my twenties and thirties,

like most people, I was expecting to marry one day. In fact, during this period I twice began to develop a relationship with a lady who I thought might be God's choice of a life partner for me. But when the time came to make a decision, I can best explain it by saying that I lacked an assurance from God that he meant me to go forward. So I drew back. And when that had happened twice, I naturally began to believe that God meant me to remain single. I'm now seventy-six and well and truly 'on the shelf!' Looking back, with the benefit of hindsight, I think I know why. I could never have traveled or written as extensively as I have done if I had had the responsibilities of a wife and family.[7]

Alone but Never Alone

Not every Christian feels called to a life of singleness as did John Stott. While the vast majority of Christians do eventually get married, we all start out being single. We all have the opportunity, for a few years at least, to serve God with the kind of undistracted devotion that Paul extols. We can step into ministry more easily than our married brothers and sisters; we are able, as Susan Foh described earlier, to "spend more time in the Lord's service—leading or attending Bible studies, staying late after work to talk to that fellow-worker with a problem." For the majority of us, these opportunities to serve God more freely will not last forever; we should make the most of them while we can.

It is worth noting that secular writers have also commented on the benefits that accrue to singles by virtue of their ability to devote themselves to different priorities than married folk can. In his book *Solitude: A Return to the Self*, author and psychiatrist Anthony Storr explores "solitude and its role in the life of creative, fulfilled individuals." His introduction quotes the great historian Edward Gibbon: "Conversation enriches the understanding, but solitude is the school of genius; and the uniformity of a work denotes the hand of a single artist." Storr then comments,

> Gibbon is surely right. The majority of poets, novelists, composers, and, to a lesser extent, of painters and sculptors, are bound to spend a great deal of their time alone, as Gibbon himself did. Current wisdom, especially that propagated by the various schools of psychoanalysis, assumes that man is a social being who needs the companionship and affection of other human beings from cradle to grave. It is widely believed that interpersonal relationships of an intimate kind are the chief, if not the only, source of human happiness. Yet the lives of creative individuals often seem to run counter to this assumption. For example, many of the world's greatest thinkers have not reared families or formed close personal ties. This is true of Descartes, Newton, Locke, Pascal, Spinoza, Kant, Liebniz, Schopenhauer, Nietzsche, Kierkegaard, and Wittenstein. Some of these men of genius had transient affairs with other men or women; others, like Newton, remained celibate. But none of them married, and most lived alone for the greater part of their lives.[8]

If and when we do get married, we should not regard matrimony as a higher state and singleness as something we are well out of. We have just seen that the Bible affirms and even exalts singleness. Conversely, if we go through life unmarried, taking advantage of the opportunities that this state provides for greater service to God, we should not regard it as a higher experience and marriage as a bullet we did well to dodge. Only forty years after Paul wrote to the

Corinthians, Clement of Rome sent them a letter apparently addressing this problem, saying, "He who is continent must not put on airs. He must recognize that his self-control is a gift from another."[9] Or as another writer put it, "It is better to be humble without being celibate than to be celibate without being humble."[10] God has designed both single-ness and marriage and has purposes for them.

Anchorite or Cenobite?

Are you an anchorite or a cenobite? Do you desire to be left alone to pursue God in utter solitude, or do you crave to be part of a social fabric? We might well ask the question of Jesus. We have already observed that significant events in His life took place while He was alone in the wilderness. Which classification would best describe Him?

Consider the evidence.

- Jesus had come to Capernaum to teach in the synagogue. He had caused evil spirits to come out of bodies. He had cured many sick and demon-possessed people. That night, He and James and John stayed at the home of Andrew and Simon. In the morning, Simon arose and went to look for Jesus, but he was not in the place where he had been the night before. Mark tells us that "very early in the morning, while it was still dark, Jesus got up, left the house and went off to a solitary place, where he prayed."[11]
- After leaving Capernaum, Jesus had traveled through Judea, returned to Capernaum, and then traveled back to Galilee. He withdrew by himself and prayed all night, alone before God. He was about to select twelve out of the many people who followed Him—twelve who would be closest to Him, twelve who would travel with Him and into whom He would pour His life, twelve disciples who would become His apostles, His "called out ones."

- Jesus' cousin, John the Baptist, had just been murdered. Herod's niece had danced so well for him on his birthday that he offered her whatever she wanted. Her mother, Herodias, was angry with John because he spoke out against the immoral relationship between Herod and Herodias, who was the wife of Herod's brother Philip. She instructed her daughter to ask for John's head, and Herod granted her wish. The disciples of Jesus claimed John's body and told Jesus what had happened. Hearing the news, Jesus "withdrew by boat privately to a solitary place."[12]
- The time of Jesus' death was drawing near, and He knew it. He and His disciples had celebrated Passover together and afterward had gone to Gethsemane. Jesus drew apart from them to pray. He knew what was about to happen, and while prepared to submit to the will of the Father, He nevertheless prayed fervently that He might be spared the horror of the crucifixion that awaited Him.

Many times, Jesus withdrew from a large group and repaired to a smaller one. Sometimes He withdrew from the multitudes to be with the Twelve. Sometimes He withdrew from the Twelve to be with the three. And sometimes He withdrew even from the three to be by Himself. Jesus needed time to be alone with the Father. Alone in prayer. Undistracted. Focused. Concentrating. But Jesus was not a monk. He did not live consistently as either an anchorite—completely alone as a hermit—or as a cenobite—in a community composed only of those with similar beliefs. His times of aloneness and solitude punctuated His times of teaching, healing, and ministering. Jesus' alone times enhanced His public ministry rather than replacing it or defining it. And He spent time not only with His followers but also with harlots, adulterers, tax collectors, lepers, the demon-possessed, Roman soldiers, religious leaders, and fishermen.

The earliest monks sought God in complete solitude, giving their whole lives to the pursuit. But often, it seems, they abandoned the world that Jesus came to save, pursuing holiness as recluses, with no seeming benefit to anyone. Is that what God intended? In many ways, we might wish to withdraw, monklike, to a safe place populated only by others who love God and then give our lives fully to the pursuit of righteousness. And sometimes we come close to doing just. We can become so insular, either as individuals or in Christian organizations, that our experiences and interactions rarely extend beyond the safety of our Christian enclave.

Modern Christians struggle with both anchoritic and cenobitic impulses. We stress the value of anchoritic "quiet times," when we can withdraw each day in solitude for prayer and Bible reading. We emphasize the need to go on cenobitic "retreats," withdrawing from the wider world and gathering into a small community of like-minded folk for fellowship and encouragement. Those experiences can be valuable. But we are also called to penetrate the world as *agent provocateurs* of a spiritual kingdom. In order to be the "salt" that arrests corruption and spoilage and the "light" that illuminates things so that they may be seen clearly, we need to enter an environment that is decaying and dark. To minister to others, we need to be with others. As singles, we have more opportunities to do this than at any other time in life. But we need to strike a balance, just as Jesus did, between time spent alone in solitude with the Father and time spent mixing it up in the hurly-burly of life.

The German pastor and theologian Dietrich Bonhoeffer brilliantly illustrates this balance in his classic work *Life Together.* (Bonhoeffer, incidentally, never married. He died at the age of 39, executed on April 9, 1945, in the Nazi concentration camp at Flossenbürg.) He wrote,

Let him who cannot be alone beware of community. He will only do harm to himself and to the community. Alone you stood before God when he called you; alone you had to answer that call; alone you had to struggle and pray; and alone you will die and give an account to God. You cannot escape from yourself; for God has singled you out. If you refuse to be alone you are rejecting Christ's call to you, and you can have no part in the community of those who are called. "The challenge of death comes to us all, and no one can die for another. Everyone must fight his own battle with death by himself, alone. . . . I will not be with you then, nor you with me" (Luther).[13]

But then he offers a counterbalance:

Let him who is not in community beware of being alone. Into the community you were called, the call was not meant for you alone; in the community of the called you bear your cross, you struggle, you pray. You are not alone, even in death, and on the Last Day you will be only one member of the great congregation of Jesus Christ. If you scorn the fellowship of the brethren, you reject the call of Jesus Christ, and thus your solitude can only be hurtful to you. "If I die, then I am not alone in death; if I suffer they [the fellowship] suffer with me" (Luther).[14]

We need this balance in our own lives. But because I think we emphasize community more and neglect solitude, perhaps we need to reexamine aloneness and consider its benefit to our walk with our Lord. We often lump this aloneness together with our singleness, scorning them both as hindrances to our walk. We are afraid that loneliness might be the partner of aloneness, and we fear that embracing aloneness even slightly will cause loneliness to become permanent and overwhelming. But that is wrong. Regardless of whether we are married, in full-time ministry, or have graduated from seminary, we need to embrace this process of "solitary refinement" and let God use it in the process of growing us into the likeness of His Son. Solitary refinement is not solitary confinement. Singleness is not a life sentence to loneliness. We need to learn to be alone with God. We need to learn not to fear our singleness but view it as an opportunity to draw close to God and to serve each other. Consider the words of St. Francis de Sales:

> Devotion ought to be practised differently by the gentleman, by the artisan, by the servant, by the prince, by the widow, by the daughter, by the wife; and not only so, but the practice of devotion must be accomodated to the strength, to the affairs, and to the duties of each one individually. I ask you . . . would it be proper for a bishop to wish to be solitary like the Carthusians? And if the married were to have no wish to lay by more than the Capuchins, and the artisan were to be in church all day like the religious, and the religious were to be always exposed to all sorts of interruptions for the service of his neighbour like the bishop, would not such devotion be ridiculous, disorderly, and intolerable?
>
> It is an error, nay rather a heresy to wish to banish the devout life from the army, from the workshop, from the courts of princes, from the households of married folk. It is true . . . that devotion of a kind which is purely contemplative, monastic and religious cannot be practised in these callings; but besides these three kinds of devotion, there are many others, which are suitable for leading to perfection

those whose lives are spent in secular avocations. . . . It has even happened that many have lost perfection in solitude . . . and have preserved it amidst the multitude. . . . Lot, says St. Gregory, who was so chaste in the city, defiled himself in solitude. Wherever we are, we may and ought to aspire to the perfect life.[15]

Consider This

1. Do you struggle with loneliness? Does fear of being lonely make you dislike being alone?
2. In what parts of your life do you currently have solitude that is spiritually beneficial? How would you like to change that?
3. Can you think of areas in which you could use the greater freedom and flexibility of singleness more effectively in the service of God?

chapter ten

A Psalter for Psingles

The delightful study of the Psalms has yielded me boundless profit and ever-growing pleasure; common gratitude constrains me to communicate to others a portion of the benefit, with the prayer that it may induce them to search further for themselves. That I have nothing better of my own to offer upon this peerless book is to me matter of deepest regret; that I have anything whatever to present is subject for devout gratitude to the Lord of grace. I have done my best, but, conscious of many defects, I heartily wish I could have done far better.

—C. H. Spurgeon, *The Treasury of David*

In times of turmoil and distress, and in times of exultation and exuberance, King David sought the Lord in prayer and poetry. He (and others) composed the collection of Hebrew poems that have come down to us as the book of Psalms. The Psalms are remarkable for their honest portrayal of the composer's utter surrender before God, for their frank declaration of sin and guilt and the desire for forgiveness, and for their joyous, worshipful praise of God's majesty and glory.

Generation after generation has turned to the Psalms for solace, for comfort, and for encouragement. Our single years provide many opportunities for us to seek refuge there. As we struggle with the pain of rejection, as we sort through the conflicts and disagreements that plague every relationship, or as we heal from the hurts inflicted by another, we, too, may turn to the Psalms and find there a balm for our pain.

But be forewarned! We may find conviction there, too— an honest heart open before God cannot help but see its own failings, its own self-absorption, and its own inconstancy as the psalmist reveals the same characteristics in his own. We might not leave some of these psalms with a warm, fuzzy feeling, but we will leave with hearts that have a renewed commitment to obey, seek, and serve God; hearts broken before Him that He might restore them; and hearts primed to revel in His splendor. And ultimately, as our hearts are open before Him and we offer to Him our innermost thoughts and deepest secrets, as we acknowledge that He knows us better than we know ourselves, we will find that any burdens pressing upon us are lifted by One who is stronger and loves to carry the load.

Psalm 1

How blessed is the man who does not walk
in the counsel of the wicked,
Nor stand in the path of sinners,
Nor sit in the seat of scoffers!
But his delight is in the law of the LORD,
And in His law he meditates day and night.
He will be like a tree firmly planted by streams of water,
Which yields its fruit in its season
And its leaf does not wither;
And in whatever he does, he prospers. (vv. 1–3)

Once, every schoolchild knew Joyce Kilmer's famous verse— "I think that I shall never see a poem lovely as a tree." A tree in its full glory is indeed a beautiful thing—strong, leafy limbs weighted down with fruit. I well remember the grapefruit trees in my grandmother's backyard, so heavy with grapefruit that some branches nearly touched the ground. By contrast, a sickly tree is a sad sight—blighted, withered, a confusion of dying sticks.

God promises to make us like strong trees—well-nourished and bursting with plump fruit and foliage. But does this result come with no effort on our part? The psalmist says that blessing results from a combination of choosing to do certain things and choosing not to do other things. We are to associate ourselves with what pleases God and dissociate ourselves from what does not please Him. We are to wrap our minds around God's laws—His precepts, principles, and prescriptions. We are to think about them continually. We are not to commit ourselves to those who don't do so.

Paul says in 1 Thessalonians that he was "continually" remembering in prayer the love, labor, and endurance of the Thessalonians. A professor of New Testament Greek once told me that the word *continually* is used by other Greek writers to describe a nagging cough. Someone so afflicted does not cough without interruption; but they find themselves coughing every so often, again and again throughout the day. I've never been able to confirm the professor's claim, but this picture of what it means to be continually in prayer or in thought about something stuck with me. The psalmist likely had something like this in mind when he wrote of meditating "day and night" upon the law of the Lord.

Walking. Standing. Sitting. These three terms express very different levels of activity, but engaging in any one of them with respect to "the counsel of the wicked," "the path of sinners," or "the seat of scoffers" brings us into association with those who do not cherish the law of God. As singles, we have many opportunities to choose with whom we will associate and identify. Choosing not to associate with those who do not honor God can cost us, and such a choice might seem to push us farther away from a mate, a family, and happiness. But God promises that if we choose to follow His path, He will honor that choice. He will not leave us unfulfilled, to wither away in frustration, to be unfruitful in our lives, or to die of thirst. He will bless us and make us prosper.

Psalm 4

Answer me when I call, O God of my righteousness!
You have relieved me in my distress;
Be gracious to me and hear my prayer.

O sons of men, how long will my honor become a
    reproach?
How long will you love what is worthless and aim at
    deception?
But know that the Lord has set apart the godly man for
    Himself;
The Lord hears when I call to Him. (vv. 1–3)

When we are lonely and hurting from the pain that single-ness can inflict, we may cry out to God as well, calling for Him to answer us. When we do so, do we recognize Him as the "God of my righteousness"? Do we acknowledge that what we have comes from Him? When we ask Him to re-lieve our distress, to extend His grace, and to hear our prayers, are we confident that He can and will do so? Do we really believe that He will do what He says?

There is a difference between those whom God has set apart for Himself and the rest of the world. There should be a difference in our lives, especially in our love-lives. It is there, indeed, that our honor may become a reproach. The purity with which we conduct the romantic parts of our lives is, as in all other aspects of our lives, a testimony to Him whom we serve. We are often surrounded by people who love what is worthless, who deceive to get what they love, who seek the wrong things from a relationship, and who value the things that are desirable in the eyes of man rather than in the eyes of the Lord. Let us examine ourselves—do we treat those whom we date in a manner that is worthy of God? Do we honor our own bodies and those of others in a manner that is worthy of the Lord? Do we value the things that are lasting and of eternal significance? Or do we value the things that are worthless? Do we treat each other honestly? Or do we, too, practice deception? God has set us apart for Himself. Does our attitude toward love reflect that calling?

> Tremble, and do not sin;
> Meditate in your heart upon your bed, and be still.
>
> Offer the sacrifices of righteousness,
> And trust in the LORD.
>
> Many are saying, "Who will show us any good?"
> Lift up the light of Your countenance upon us, O LORD!
> You have put gladness in my heart,
> More than when their grain and new wine abound.
> In peace I will both lie down and sleep,
> For You alone, O LORD, make me to dwell in safety.
>   (vv. 4–8)

When we are lonely and hurting from the struggles of singleness, how are we to respond? We are to tremble before the awesome majesty of a mighty God. We are to shun sin. We are to meditate and let His stillness envelope our hearts. We are to place our lives on the altar before Him—we are to sacrifice everything. We are to trust in Him.

What will He do? He will put gladness in our hearts. He will permit us to walk in the peace of His assurance rather than in the pain of unmet need. His provision might not take the form we wish, but He assures us peace—peace enough to lie down and sleep in the face of the enemy, as He gave to David. By His provision, we may dwell in safety—secure in the knowledge that our lives are in His hands—including our love-lives.

Psalm 6

Be gracious to me, O Lord, for I am pining away;
Heal me, O Lord, for my bones are dismayed.
And my soul is greatly dismayed;
But You, O Lord—how long? . . .

I am weary with my sighing;
Every night I make my bed swim,
I dissolve my couch with my tears.
My eye has wasted away with grief;
It has become old because of all my adversaries. . . .

For the Lord has heard the voice of my weeping.
The Lord has heard my supplication,
The Lord receives my prayer. (vv. 2–3, 6–9)

How often do we as singles cry out, "O Lord—how long?" How long before I really fall in love? How long before I meet the right person? How long before I am happily married, even as all of my friends are? How often do we have the experience of wearing ourselves out with our own sighing? Of crying ourselves to sleep late into the night? Of fighting the feeling that we are of no value because no one loves us? For us, just as for David, the solace is found in knowing that the Lord is not deaf to our weeping, that He hears, accepts, and answers our prayers. But we must pray! We must turn the weeping into supplication. We must let the tears and the sighing speak our pain to God. We must again lay our troubles and longings before Him. We must believe that He hears prayer and will answer, although His answer might not be our answer and His timing might not be our timing. We need to rest assured that our prayers are heard; our suffering is not unnoticed.

Psalm 19

The law of the LORD is perfect, restoring the soul;
The testimony of the LORD is sure, making wise the
    simple.
The precepts of the LORD are right, rejoicing the heart;
The commandment of the LORD is pure, enlightening the
    eyes.
The fear of the LORD is clean, enduring forever;
The judgments of the LORD are true; they are righteous
    altogether.
They are more desirable than gold, yes, than much fine
    gold;
Sweeter also than honey and the drippings of the
    honeycomb. (vv. 7-10)

Are these things not also ultimately more desirable than the pleasures of marriage and of family? Are they not sweeter than the love of a beautiful woman or a handsome man? To say otherwise treads the border of idolatry. Not that marriage, family, or a mate is wrong or undesirable—not that at all! But by contrast, the things of the Lord are of far greater value. Paul counted all his accomplishments and achievements as "rubbish" (literally, "excrement") in contrast to Christ—not because they were inherently worthless but because Christ was worth infinitely more.

Unless we see that truth, unless we learn to ascribe value by God's standards, we cannot appreciate anything as God intended it. Do you long to be married, to have a mate to appreciate and be appreciated by? Do you wish to derive pleasure in the fullness of such a relationship? Then you must see these things from God's perspective. For only when love and marriage, or anything else, are viewed from His perspective are they able to truly fulfill the heart that belongs to the Lord.

Do you wish for a "whole soul," for wisdom, for a glad heart, for clear spiritual vision, for character that endures, for true righteousness? Then cherish the things of the Lord: His law, His testimony, His precepts, His commandments, His judgments, and His awe-inspiring fearsomeness. Only when He is given His proper place in one's life—and one's love-life—only when He sits on the throne, is fulfillment possible.

Psalm 25

To You, O LORD, I lift up my soul.
O my God, in You I trust. . . .

Make me know Your ways, O LORD;
Teach me Your paths.
Lead me in Your truth and teach me,
For You are the God of my salvation;
For You I wait all the day. . . .

All the paths of the LORD are lovingkindness and truth
To those who keep His covenant and His testimonies.
   (vv. 1–2, 4–5, 10)

Do we really trust in God not only when we get our way but also when getting what we want seems impossible? Do we trust Him when God clearly and finally shuts the door to something or someone we wanted and there is no hope of reopening it? Sometimes we convince ourselves that even though we can't get it for ourselves, maybe God will work a miracle and provide it. But can we go further and trust that if He refuses to provide something it must be for our best, and then let it go? Can we believe that every denial is an invitation to an even greater blessing?

Do we really want God to make His ways known to us? To make His paths clear to us? What if the path is one we would rather not follow? Do we still want to be taught His path? And what about being led? Are we truly willing for God to lead? Often it seems that we want God to bless us as we choose to go our own way—but that is not the way it works. He leads; we follow.

What about waiting? When biological alarms are sounding and we panic over the apparent indifference of God to our dilemma, can we still be patient and wait on Him? Are we content to wait on His timing, not just all of the day but all of our lives?

Psalm 27

> The LORD is my light and my salvation;
> Whom shall I fear?
> The LORD is the defense of my life;
> Whom shall I dread? (v. 1)

Perhaps for us a more pertinent question is "What shall I dread?" Shall I dread being alone for the rest of my life? Shall I dread never having the things that others have, the things that conventional wisdom says make life happy and fulfilling? Shall I fear the loneliness of my later years as my friends all marry and are consumed with the responsibilities of their families? In the midst of that dread, can we understand that we need not fear because the Lord is our light, our salvation, and our defense?

> One thing I have asked from the LORD, that I shall seek:
> That I may dwell in the house of the LORD all the days of
>   my life,
> To behold the beauty of the LORD,
> And to meditate in His temple.
> For in the day of trouble He will conceal me in His
>   tabernacle;
> In the secret place of His tent He will hide me;
> He will lift me up on a rock. (vv. 4–5)

Is that true for us? If we could ask but one thing of the Lord, would it be this? Or would it be a mate? A family? A successful career? An impact on society? Material comfort? Influence? Is our foremost desire to dwell in His house all the days of our lives? There is no safer dwelling place. When trouble comes, is there any place better for us to be hidden than with Him? The nicest house inhabited by the most loving spouse and the most beautiful family is no substitute.

Psalm 36

> Your lovingkindness, O LORD, extends to the heavens,
> Your faithfulness reaches to the skies.
> Your righteousness is like the mountains of God;
> Your judgments are like a great deep.
> O LORD, You preserve man and beast.
> How precious is Your lovingkindness, O God!
> And the children of men take refuge in the shadow of
>   Your wings.
> They drink their fill of the abundance of Your house;
> And You give them to drink of the river of Your
>   delights.

For with You is the fountain of life;
In Your light we see light. (vv. 5–9)

As we see our hopes dashed and our expectations unmet, there is perhaps no greater truth of which we need to remind ourselves than that God is a God of lovingkindness, of loyal-love, of *chesed,* to use the Hebrew word. He is a God who undertakes covenants and fulfills them utterly in His loyal-love—He spared not even His Son to fulfill His promises to us. We need to remind ourselves continually that His lovingkindness is real. It is not merely a theological concept or a subject for a Hebrew word study. This love is boundless; it reaches to the heavens. It is by His righteousness that we are guaranteed His loyal-love, and His righteousness is solid and unmovable, like a mountain. His judgments are like a great deep, vast and unfathomable. Although we are totally undeserving, He has chosen to extend His loyal-love to us. It is precious. In it we find refuge and safety. In it we are provided for in abundance. In it we are delighted. In it there is life and light. It is easy for us to miss these things as we focus on what we do not have and envy what others have. It is easy for us to rail against God for cruelly depriving us, but to do so is to miss the incredible bounty that His loyal-love provides. To do so is tragically to miss the tangibility of the loyal-love that He extends to us.

Psalm 37

Trust in the LORD and do good;
Dwell in the land and cultivate faithfulness.
Delight yourself in the LORD;
And He will give you the desires of your heart.
Commit your way to the LORD,
Trust also in Him, and He will do it. (vv. 3–5)

Action and outcome. Here they are paired in perfect harmony. What are the desires of your heart? To be married? To have a significant other? To have a family? To live a godly life? To share your love of Jesus with others? God offers to give us the desires of our hearts. But what must we do? We must "trust in the LORD . . . do good . . . dwell in the land"—minister as faithful servants wherever God puts us; "cultivate faithfulness"—choose to believe the promises of God; "commit your way to the Lord"—resolve in our hearts to follow Him wherever He leads, even if to us it makes no sense. How often do we whine and complain before God because He has not given us the desires of our hearts? Yet we fail to admit to ourselves that we have done none of these things that He asks.

Psalm 55

Cast your burden upon the LORD and He will sustain you;
He will never allow the righteous to be shaken. (v. 22)

How often we fail to do this—in the midst of turmoil, simply cast our burden upon the Lord! We choose instead to work things out on our own—to manipulate circumstances to get attention, to get a date, to get a commitment. Then we connive to keep from losing those things. We worry. We fret. We scheme. Instead, we must simply lay our burden at His feet. We must rely on Him to sustain and uphold us.

Psalm 71

But as for me, I will hope continually,
And will praise You yet more and more.
My mouth shall tell of Your righteousness
And of Your salvation all day long;
For I do not know the sum of them. (vv. 14–15)

After every unfulfilled expectation, after every failed romance, it is difficult indeed to continue to hope. It is agony to suffer unfulfilled love and mourn the loss while hoping that when God closes one door He will open another. But that is what we must do. God is the One in whom we may hope continually. We are assured of His loyal-love and may make it the basis of our hope. Even when our present desires are not met, we must praise Him, we must tell of His righteousness, of His goodness, of the amazing grace by which He has saved us. We do not know the sum of His glories or of His blessings. We do know, however, that they are beyond counting, that He pours out His grace upon us beyond measure. And that is something in which truly to rejoice.

Psalm 73

Behold, these are the wicked;
And always at ease, they have increased in wealth.
Surely in vain I have kept my heart pure
And washed my hands in innocence;
For I have been stricken all day long
And chastened every morning. (vv. 12–14)

When we lose someone to another, perhaps it is to this psalm that we should come. It is easy to think of the persons who got what we wanted as the enemy, as "the wicked." Although they probably do not deserve that epithet, it is still hard to see someone else prosper—get what we wanted—while we remain impoverished. It is particularly hard when our loss may be due to our obedience to the Lord, when we have tried our hardest to pursue romance in a manner that honors both Him and the one we want, and we lose out to someone who does not honor Him. We cry out to God, "Lord, what is wrong here? Have I not obeyed You? Have I not prayed? Have I not sought to walk in Your will? And yet, this other person, who does not honor You as I do, has succeeded where I have failed. Is this fair?" In all areas of our lives we struggle with knowing that obedience to God may require us to give up something that we want very much.

> My flesh and my heart may fail,
> But God is the strength of my heart and my portion
> forever.
> For, behold, those who are far from You will perish;
> You have destroyed all those who are unfaithful to You.
> But as for me, the nearness of God is my good;
> I have made the Lord God my refuge,
> That I may tell of all Your works. (vv. 26–28)

This must be our solace when we feel deprived by our obedience to God. From Him is our strength drawn—the strength to overcome the loss and remain obedient to Him in the face of a powerful incentive to compromise. Our provision and our life are found in Him; those who do not honor Him, He will destroy. The nearness of another person is something most of us desire—an intimate relationship with a husband or wife is indeed something worthwhile for which to long. But more glorious still is that God offers us nearness to Him, and it is only through that nearness that the "shadow-nearness" of a husband or wife has real meaning.

Psalm 84

> For the Lord God is a sun and shield;
> The Lord gives grace and glory;
> No good thing does He withhold from those who walk
> uprightly.
> O Lord of hosts,
> How blessed is the man who trusts in You! (vv. 11–12)

"'No good thing does He withhold.' But isn't marriage a good thing? Why, then, am I not married? Isn't dating a good thing? Why, then, is no one interested in dating me? Isn't expressing love and honor for another person a good thing? Then why does no one express those things for me, or respond when I express them?" These are hard questions. God promises not to withhold what is good, but when we are not in possession of good things, what are we to think?

What are the good things mentioned here? God is a sun. He is radiant. He provides light to illuminate, and warmth to sustain life. God is a shield. He protects us. He wards off that which would cause harm. God is a giver of grace. God is a giver of glory. Can we say that He has withheld those from us? Never!

"No good thing does He withhold from those who walk uprightly." Let us examine ourselves. Do we walk uprightly? Do we seek righteousness? Do we long to be holy, to be sanctified, no matter what the cost? Are we willing to separate ourselves from the unclean things to make possible that holiness?

"How blessed is the man who trusts in You!" Let us examine ourselves again. Do we trust Him? Not just say that we trust Him with our tongues, so that men may hear, but truly trust Him with all our hearts? Do we trust Him to provide a husband or a wife if that is a good thing? Are we content to accept that He may not provide because having a spouse at this particular time may not be a good thing for us?

Psalm 86

Teach me Your way, O Lord;
I will walk in Your truth;
Unite my heart to fear Your name.

> I will give thanks to You, O Lord my God, with all my
>   heart,
> And will glorify Your name forever.
> For Your lovingkindness toward me is great,
> And You have delivered my soul from the depths of
>   Sheol. (vv. 11–13)

Is there any greater prayer that we as single men and women could pray? *Teach me Your way, O Lord.* Make it specific and personal: "Teach me Your way in relationships, O Lord. Teach me what a marriage is for. Teach me how to love and honor my spouse, both as a mate and as a brother or sister in Christ. Teach me to reject the teachings of the world, so sadly perverted by evil, so tragically twisted in what they say about men and women. Teach me to love as You love. Teach me to honor as You honor. Teach me not to settle for what passes in this world as love, but to know and to long for the standard that You have set. Teach me Your way, O Lord."

I will walk in Your truth. "You are teaching me Your way, Lord; I want to act on it. I want it not only to permeate my mind but also to penetrate my heart. I want my life to be transformed by living out Your truth. I do not want to be a spiritual tadpole—all head and no heart. I want to express Your love to others. Knowing what true love is, I want to pour it out. I want to go places, Lord; I will walk where You lead. I will walk in Your truth, O Lord."

Unite my heart to fear Your name. "Many things pull at me, Lord. I want to follow You. I want to be obedient, but my heart hears many voices. I hear You. I hear my parents and relatives. I hear my friends. I hear the world. I hear those who honor You. I hear those who do not honor You. Since childhood, I have been taught to expect certain things from life and to try my best to get them. I have learned that my life will be a failure if I do not. If I do not marry, if

I do not raise "good kids," if I do not succeed in my career, I will be a failure. I am afraid, O Lord. Afraid that somehow I will fail, that my life will be a ruin if I do not answer all of the voices in my heart. Unite my heart, Lord, to fear Your name. Make the voices one voice—Yours. Let me hear it clearly, and let my heart respond in fear and reverence to You.

"Whatever happens, Lord, I will thank You. Not casually, but from the depths of my heart. Not trivially, not because You have given me what I wanted, but because You are God, You are my Lord, worthy of praise. Your love is loyal. You have saved me and blanketed me with Your loyallove. Forever will I glorify Your name—whether single or married, happy or unhappy, feeling fulfilled or unfulfilled."

Psalm 101

I will sing of lovingkindness and justice,
To You, O Lord, I will sing praises.
I will give heed to the blameless way.
When will You come to me?
I will walk within my house in the integrity of my heart.
I will set no worthless thing before my eyes;
I hate the work of those who fall away;
It shall not fasten its grip on me.
A perverse heart shall depart from me;
I will know no evil. (vv. 1–4)

Proverbs 4:23 is often quoted to singles: "Watch over your heart with all diligence, for from it flow the springs of life." The content of our lives reflects the character of our hearts. Conversely, the character of our hearts will determine the content of our lives. As singles, do we "guard our hearts"? Do we take seriously that watchful duty? Have we determined that we will "give heed to the blameless way," that we will walk in the integrity of our hearts? That we will set nothing worthless before our eyes, that we will set our hearts upon no unrighteous goals? Are we steadfast in our commitment to keep our hearts from growing perverse, to "know no evil"? It is easy for us to say "yes"—but do our lives show it?

Psalm 127

> Unless the Lord builds the house,
> They labor in vain who build it;
> Unless the Lord guards the city,
> The watchman keeps awake in vain. (v. 1)

We often get into the greatest trouble in relationships because we follow our own agenda rather than God's. There is a big difference between "stepping out in faith" and "steamrollering in faith." Sometimes we ignore the distinction. It is easy to construct not just a house but a veritable skyscraper of expectations when we become interested in someone. We imagine just how the relationship should proceed, what should happen and when, and become discouraged, petulant, or angry when things don't work out that way. When we start down that path, we would do well to heed this verse. Whether pursuing a particular relationship or aiming at marriage in general, unless we can honestly say that the Lord is in it, that we have prayed over what we should do and with whom, and that we are following His lead, our efforts are futile. Too often we jump blindly into relationships without prayer, falling to our knees only when things begin to fall apart. We need to be in prayer before stepping out. We need to be assured that it is the Lord who "builds the house."

Psalm 141

Set a guard, O LORD, over my mouth;
Keep watch over the door of my lips.
Do not incline my heart to any evil thing,
To practice deeds of wickedness
With men who do iniquity;
And do not let me eat of their delicacies.

Let the righteous smite me in kindness and reprove me;
It is oil upon the head;
Do not let my head refuse it,
For still my prayer is against their wicked deeds.
   (vv. 3–5)

In examining earlier psalms, we considered that the desire for integrity and personal righteousness should be central in all aspects of our lives, but especially in our love-lives. Here David asks God to help him in his struggle against his desire to do evil. But David goes further—he asks God to use the righteous to rebuke him when he goes astray. Are we willing to do this for each other? Are we willing to approach each other and speak the truth in love? Are we willing, "laying aside falsehood, [to] speak truth each one of you with his neighbor, for we are members of one another"?[1] Do we feel free to confront those whom we love when they are making bad choices? When we do, is it really out of love and not out of anger or self-righteousness?

Turn it around. Are we willing to have others "smite us in kindness"? When we are confronted by another, how do we respond? Are we defensive? Are we angry at having our actions or motives questioned? Do we counterattack with a list of what the other person has done wrong? David illustrates what our response should be. He invites it. He knows that it is for his own good and in his best interest. He rejoices in it: "It is oil upon the head; Do not let my head refuse it." Reproof, when motivated by a godly concern, is an anointing, an act conferring honor upon the recipient. For someone to risk provoking a hostile response by confronting another in love is indeed an expression of the love of Christ.

Psalm 150

Praise the LORD!
Praise God in His sanctuary;
Praise Him in His mighty expanse.
Praise Him for His mighty deeds;
Praise Him according to His excellent greatness. . . .
Praise the LORD! (vv. 1–2, 6)

May it ever be so! Whether single or married, alone or with others, wealthy or impoverished. Whether free or imprisoned, ill or healthy, feeling satisfied or unsatisfied—let us praise the Lord!

Consider This

1. Pick three psalms that were not discussed in this chapter. You might do so using your birthday. For example, if you were born on 2/24/75, read Psalm 2, Psalm 24, and Psalm 75. Keep a notebook handy and jot down your own thoughts as you read these psalms and reflect upon what is revealed in them. Consider how the psalmist's words might apply to the issues with which you are currently dealing as a single person. If those three psalms don't strike you as being relevant to the single life, pick three others.
2. Reflect on the areas where you struggle as a single person and compose your own psalms. Let each psalm focus on only one particular issue or aspect of your life, and

develop your thoughts and feelings about that issue in depth in that psalm.

chapter eleven

Finishing Well

This is not the end.
It is not even the beginning of the end.
But it is, perhaps, the end of the beginning.
—Winston Churchill,
Speech at the Mansion House,
November 10, 1942

Not long ago, I attended a pastor's conference held in conjunction with the fiftieth anniversary of Peninsula Bible Church in Palo Alto, California. The program included talks from several prominent people who have been involved with the ministry of that church over the years, including Chuck Swindoll, who was an intern there in 1961. During a panel discussion held toward the end of the day, the speakers were asked if there was anything they wanted to say to each other before taking questions from the audience. Dr. Swindoll looked around at the other speakers on the platform, whom he had known for years, and said, "I'm so encouraged these guys are finishing well. . . . The longer I live, the more I appreciate the fact that they love the Lord more now than the last time I saw them."

I couldn't help but wonder: Will my peer group be able to say the same thing of each other twenty or thirty years down the road? What should our lives look like now if we want to end up "finishing well"? In particular, how do we negotiate our single years in a way that will enable us at the end of our lives to look back and say, "I'm finishing well"?

First, we might make sure that we have a scriptural framework for evaluating our single years, our dating practices, our desires for marriage, and our expectations of a spouse. The intention of this book has been to provide at least a head start in that direction. But where do we go from here? Even if we agree at an intellectual or theological level that God loves us and is adequate to meet our needs, does that lessen our longing? Does it lessen our pain when our love is rejected? Does understanding God's intention for marriage and the limits He places on what we may do outside of marriage make it any easier to live within those limits? Does knowing that God intends to bless us make it any easier to wait until He does so? Does understanding our identity and knowing the source of true satisfaction make us feel any more secure and satisfied?

I think that we are bound to be discouraged if we expect our intellectual understanding of God's truth to translate immediately into emotional equanimity. Understanding and feeling are two different things. The only way for our hearts to catch up with our heads is for us to step out in faith, acting on the basis of our understanding regardless of our feelings, and trust God to close the gap. It might not be easy to do that, but it is essential. It is essential that we believe what God says about who we are and act accordingly. It is essential that we hold fast to the truth and maintain the integrity of our walk. It is essential that we act as though we believe He is sovereign and that He knows what we need and will provide it, even if we don't feel that way. As an old Puritan prayer says, "Help me to honour Thee by believing before I feel, for great is the sin if I make feeling a cause of faith."[1]

There is no easy way to navigate through relationships

or the lack thereof. There is no detailed map that charts a passage from singleness to matrimony. Maybe it is good that there is no such thing. If there were, we would be able to race forward on our own, thinking that we had no need of God's guidance. We often do that anyway, map or no map, plunging ahead on our own course until eventually we get lost and cry out to Him for help. We would be much better off throwing away our navigational aids altogether and simply trusting in His guidance day by day, situation by situation, relationship by relationship, and need by need.

I believe that each of us reaches a critical juncture in our lives as Christians, a "terrible moment" when we come to the frightening realization that belonging to Christ requires something other than attending church regularly, dropping a few dollars in the offering plate, or reciting spiritual-sounding phrases. It requires complete surrender. In that moment, we admit to ourselves that everything we depend on for survival and success is utterly futile, that in the end no effort of our own is efficacious at all. In that moment, we make a choice—depend on God halfheartedly, try to make it in our strength, and cry out to Him only when we can't; or submit to His sovereignty, trust His loyal-love, and abide in the faith that God is God and we are His children.

Singleness can be a struggle, often a very hard one. Pressures both internal and external tell us that singleness, like childhood, is a stage through which we must pass to attain maturity. We are told that something better and grander is beyond and that we are not truly fulfilled until we reach it. But that statement is misdirection. It is not singleness that we need to let go, but selfishness. It is not marriage that we need to strive toward, but obedience. If anything inhibits fulfillment, it is probably our own unwillingness to let God fulfill us where we are now, with what we have now, as the persons we are now.

We need courage in this struggle. We need courage to

ignore what the world, sometimes even the church, tells us about our worth, our happiness, our fulfillment, and the sources of these things. We need courage to ignore this input and listen in stillness to God. We need courage to believe the incredible notion that the invisible acts in the visible, that the eternal acts in the temporal, and that the infinite acts in the finite.

We need integrity in this struggle. We need integrity to adhere to God's standard and not be distracted from it. We need integrity to stand within a world, obsessed with sex and self, and testify that there is another way and that it is, in fact, the only way, regardless of whether that view is "politically correct." We need integrity to maintain steadfastly that there is absolute truth in a world in which the ability to apply "spin," to practice deception, to shade meaning through clever semantics, and to lie without giving the appearance of lying is increasingly prized. We need integrity if the affirmation of that truth is to mean more to us than the gratification of our own desires.

We need conviction in this struggle. We need to have come to that "terrible moment" and to have renounced compromise for commitment. We need to be convinced that we live in the visible manifestation of an invisible reality, in the present shadow of a future glory, in the temporal display of a timeless truth. We need the conviction that God is utterly faithful to fulfill the promises that He makes. We need conviction to walk in obedience even when it means giving up things we want. We need conviction to choose the path of holiness even when our emotions cry out in rebellion, even when to do so makes us feel miserable and unfulfilled.

We need prayer in this struggle. We need prayer as the means of responding to feeling miserable and unfulfilled. When we feel that way, we need to confess those feelings to our Father in prayer and allow Him to use that process to comfort us. We need prayer to strengthen our relationship with Him who is the very source of life. We need to be able to approach Him as little children and confess our heartbreak and unsatisfied longings. We need prayer as a means of moment-by-moment realizing our need, confessing our need, and trusting Him to provide for our need.

We need compassion in this struggle. We need compassion to keep from gloating—intentionally or unintentionally—or believing ourselves superior when we find ourselves in love while our friends are not, or when we get married while our friends remain single. We need compassion toward those whose affections we do not reciprocate that we may treat them honorably as brothers or sisters. We need compassion toward those who spurn us to bring to fruition our eternal relationship as members of the body of Christ.

We need solitude in this struggle. We need solitude to further our relationship with Christ to draw close to Him in the quietness of our spirits, and let Him speak to us. We need time alone with our Savior to enjoy the sweet intimacy with God that Christ's death made possible. We need solitude to cultivate the stillness of heart that allows us to hear Him as He speaks softly to us, as He comforts and convicts us, and as He encourages and upholds us.

We need community in this struggle. We need each other. The community of believers is likened to the physical body for a reason. Each member has a unique role and capabilities, through which he or she contributes to the well-being of the whole. We need to support, correct, exhort, reprove, console, encourage, and uplift one another. We need to pray for and with one another. We need to appreciate each other for the unique way that God has crafted each of us. We need to honor each other and participate together in the process of growing Christlike, to build up each other through the exercise of our spiritual gifts. Whether single or married, we are part of one another.

There was a woman, not so very different from you or me, who longed to be happy—as do we. She sought that fulfillment in relationships—as often do we. She had married five times, looking for fulfillment in each man. Not finding it, she moved on to another man. She was living with a sixth man, seeking fulfillment yet again.

When this woman met Jesus at a well in Samaria, He showed her that the need she was trying to satisfy was not a physical need, an emotional need, or a need that any human relationship could meet. Hers was a spiritual need that could be filled only by Him. She thought in terms of temporary physical thirst and the satisfaction of a cool drink of water. Jesus spoke to her of the continual, deep quenching of an eternal spiritual thirst. In that moment, as Jesus declared to her that He was the promised Messiah, this woman was wrenched from the transient into the eternal. I think that this must have been her "terrible moment" when her finite comprehension of herself, of life, and of the world was confounded by a glimpse of the eternal and all of its implications—and she was forced to decide how to respond to it.

So, too, are we. Eternity has penetrated our temporary world; it is a fact that we cannot ignore. Our decision to follow Christ has eternal implications that have begun to manifest themselves here and now. We, too, have been wrenched from the transient into the eternal. We can ill afford to focus solely on the temporary, no matter how urgently it cries for our attention, no matter how attractively it promises satisfaction, and no matter how deeply we feel the fear of being passed by.

All earthly things that we think will satisfy, ultimately will not. Possessions, success, friendships, dating relationship, marriages—none of these will ultimately satisfy. The void we want them to fill, the void we hope they will fill will only be replaced by another void, because our fundamental need is for no person other than Jesus. We must look to Him first for fulfillment, for satisfaction, and for significance. Only then will any human relationship provide the measure of fulfillment, satisfaction, and significance that God intends. If we learn to seek Jesus first, we are virtually assured of "finishing well."

Notes

Chapter 1: Taxonomy

1. Philippians 1:6 NIV.
2. 1 Corinthians 6:19–20.
3. For an extended discussion of the principle that all believers are called to minister, see Ray C. Stedman, *Body Life* (Ventura, Calif.: Regal, 1972). Stedman captures the basic idea: "Throughout the Christian centuries no principle of church life has proved more revolutionary (and therefore, more bitterly fought) than the declaration of Ephesians 4 that the ultimate work of the church in the world is to be done by the saints—plain, ordinary Christians—and not by a professional clergy or a few select laymen. We must never lose the impact of the apostle Paul's statement that apostles, prophets, evangelists, and pastor-teachers exist *for the equipment of the saints, for the work of ministry, for building up of the body of Christ* (Eph. 4:12)" (87). More recent works championing this principle include William M. Easum, *Sacred Cows Make Gourmet Burgers: Ministry Anytime, Anywhere, by Anyone* (Nashville, Tenn.: Abingdon, 1995); and Os Guinness, *The Call* (Nashville, Tenn.: Word, 1998).
4. Romans 12:1–8; 1 Corinthians 12; 1 Peter 4:10–11.
5. From Hecataeus, *The History of Egypt,* as quoted in Luciano Canfora, *The Vanished Library* (Berkeley, Calif.: University of California Press, 1990), 21.
6. Jeremiah 17:9.

7. Amos 8:11.
8. 2 Timothy 3:16–17.
9. James 1:23–25.
10. Psalm 119:105.

Chapter 2: Paradigm Lost / Paradigm Regained

1. Thomas S. Kuhn, *The Structure of Scientific Revolutions* (Chicago: University of Chicago Press, 1996).
2. Romans 12:2.
3. With apologies to W. S. Gilbert and Sir Arthur Sullivan, from whose operetta *The Mikado* this line is drawn, the relevance of which will be evident as the reader presses onward.
4. Stephen Hersh, "Bliss," *Universal Press Syndicate,* 2 April 1999.
5. Lyle W. Dorsett, *A Love Observed* (Wheaton, Ill.: Harold Shaw, 1983); and George Sayer, *Jack: A Life of C. S. Lewis* (Wheaton, Ill.: Crossway, 1994).
6. With apologies to Paul Simon.
7. Robert L. Hubbard Jr., "The Book of Ruth," *New International Commentary on the Old Testament* (Grand Rapids: Eerdmans, 1988), 49.
8. Ruth 1:16–17.
9. Ruth 2:11–12.
10. Ruth 3:9.
11. Hubbard, "The Book of Ruth," 212.
12. Ruth 3:11.
13. Genesis 24:1–9.
14. Genesis 12.
15. Genesis 24:7.
16. Genesis 24:11–14.
17. Genesis 24:15–27.

Chapter 3: Satisfiction

1. Roy Baham, "Charlie's Shoes," © 1972, 1973, 1974, 1990 CBS Records, Inc., performed by Billy Walker.
2. Henry David Thoreau, *Walden and Civil Disobedience* (New York: Penguin Books, 1986), 50.
3. 1 Kings 10:6–8.

4. Ecclesiastes 1:13, 16.

5. Ecclesiastes 1:17–18.

6. Ecclesiastes 2:1, 8, 10.

7. Ecclesiastes 2:1–2.

8. Ecclesiastes 2:4–6.

9. Ecclesiastes 2:7–9.

10. Ecclesiastes 2:11.

11. R. L. Laird, G. L. Archer, and B. K. Waltke, eds., *Theological Wordbook of the Old Testament* (Chicago: Moody, 1980), 204–5.

12. Arthur Bennett, ed., *The Valley of Vision: A Collection of Puritan Prayers and Devotions* (Edinburgh: Banner of Truth Trust, 1975), 13.

13. Ecclesiastes 12:1, 6–7, 13.

14. Augustine, *The Confessions of Augustine in Modern English*, ed. Sherwood E. Wirt (Grand Rapids: Zondervan, 1986), 6.6.86.

15. Ibid., 1.1.1.

16. Blaise Pascal, *Pensees* (Baltimore: Penguin Books, 1968), 174–75.

Chapter 4: Gaining Wait

1. "We Must Wait (On the Lord)" by Randy Thomas. © Maranatha! Music. All rights reserved.

2. James Gleick, *Faster: The Acceleration of Just About Everything* (New York: Pantheon, 1999), 277.

3. Hebrews 11:1.

4. Thomas John Carlisle, *Eve and After: Old Testament Women in Portrait* (Grand Rapids: Eerdmans, 1984), 128.

5. J. Carl Laney, *First and Second Samuel* (Chicago: Moody, 1982), 17.

6. Carlisle, *Eve and After,* 67.

7. Hebrews 11:12; Genesis 15:5; 22:17.

8. Hebrews 11:13.

9. Romans 8:19, 22–23.

10. Arthur Dallimore, *Spurgeon: A New Biography* (Edinburgh: Banner of Truth, 1985), 64.

11. Tom Carter, *Spurgeon at His Best* (Grand Rapids: Baker, 1988), 215.

12. Ibid.
13. 2 Peter 3:8.

Chapter 5: "Don't Make No Sense"

1. Ruthe Stein, "Singles Seeking Religious Soul Mates," *San Francisco Chronicle,* 31 March 1992.
2. Luke 6:46 NIV.
3. Luke 6:47–49 NIV.
4. Colossians 3:1–4 NIV.
5. 1 Peter 1:13–16 NIV.
6. Romans 6:3–7 NIV.
7. Ephesians 4:17–19 NIV.
8. Ephesians 4:20–24 NIV.
9. Philippians 2:1–4 NIV.
10. Philippians 2:6–8 NIV.
11. Romans 12:10 NIV.
12. Romans 12:10 NIV.
13. Romans 12:16 NIV.
14. Romans 14:13 NIV.
15. Romans 14:19.
16. Romans 15:7.
17. Galatians 5:13 NIV.
18. Galatians 6:2.
19. Ephesians 4:32 NIV.
20. Colossians 3:9.
21. Colossians 3:13 NIV.
22. Colossians 3:16.
23. 1 Thessalonians 4:18.
24. 1 Thessalonians 5:11.
25. Hebrews 10:24.
26. James 4:11.
27. James 5:16.
28. 1 Peter 1:22.
29. 1 Peter 4:9.
30. 1 Peter 5:5.
31. Hebrews 3:12 NIV.
32. Hebrews 3:16–19 NIV.

33. Hebrews 4:1 NIV.
34. Hebrews 4:9 NIV.
35. Hebrews 4:10 NIV.

Chapter 6: The Yoke's on You

1. Names have been changed to protect privacy.
2. Galatians 6:2.
3. James 5:16.
4. 1 Thessalonians 4:18.
5. Ephesians 4:15.
6. Hebrews 10:24.
7. 2 Corinthians 6:14.
8. 1 Corinthians 2:14 NIV.
9. John 15–17.
10. Romans 6:1–2 NIV.

Chapter 7: A Commotion of Emotions

1. Bill Gillham, *Lifetime Guarantee* (Eugene, Ore.: Harvest House, 1993).
2. John 21:20–21.
3. John 21:22.
4. Matthew 6:25–34.
5. Matthew 6:7–8.
6. Luke 9:3–4.
7. Job 10:1–2.
8. Ephesians 4:31.
9. Ephesians 4:17–19.
10. Ephesians 4:20–24.
11. Ephesians 4:25–27, 29–30, 32.

Chapter 8: The Swirling Vortex of Desire

1. William J. Petersen, *Martin Luther Had a Wife* (Wheaton, Ill.: Tyndale, 1983), 24.
2. J. I. Packer, *God's Words* (Grand Rapids: Baker, 1981), 97. The references to Dr. Snaith relate to that gentleman's articles on some of these words in *A Theological Wordbook of the Bible*, ed. Alan Richardson (New York: Macmillan, 1953), 100–102.

3. Packer, *God's Words,* 169.

4. Warren W. Wiersbe, *Be Holy* (Colorado Springs: Chariot Victor, 1994), 11.

5. Jack Finegan, *The Archeology of the New Testament* (Princeton, N.J.: Princeton University Press, 1969), 120.

6. And *one* person (Jesus) on *one* day (that of His death) broke that restriction forever!

7. F. F. Bruce, *1 and 2 Thessalonians* (Waco, Tex.: Word, 1982), 82. Within the brackets, I have substituted "sexual immorality" for the corresponding Greek word *porneia,* which is what appears in the original quotation.

8. 1 Corinthians 6:13.

9. 1 Corinthians 6:18–20.

10. 2 Corinthians 12:21.

11. Ephesians 5:3, 5.

12. Colossians 3:5.

13. For an excellent discussion, see Henry W. Soltau, *The Holy Vessel and Furniture of the Tabernacle* (Grand Rapids: Kregel, 1971).

14. The name *Epiphanes* means "exalted." So tyrannical was his reign that some wags called him *Epimanes,* which means "madman."

15. "1 Maccabees 1:26–29," *The Jerusalem Bible,* Reader's ed. (Garden City, N.Y.: Doubleday, 1968), 571.

16. 2 Corinthians 4:7.

17. 2 Timothy 2:21.

18. In 1 Samuel 21:5, David requests consecrated bread from the priest Ahimelech. Before he will give it to him, Ahimelech asks David if his men have "kept themselves from women" (v. 4). David replies, "Surely women have been kept from us as previously when I set out and the vessels of the young men were holy" (v. 5). Here, *vessels* translates the Hebrew word *keli* (כְּלִי), which usually also means "vessel" in the literal sense (and is used in the preceding Leviticus 11 passage to describe a clay pot) but is also known to be used as a euphemism for genitalia. In the Septuagint, the Greek word *skeous* is used in the same sense, although in a somewhat

obscure way. See Bruce, *1 and 2 Thessalonians,* 83; C. A. Wanamaker, *Commentary on 1 and 2 Thessalonians* (Grand Rapids: Eerdmans, 1990), 152–53; and Torleif Elgvin, "'To Master His Own Vessel': 1 Thess. 4:4 in Light of New Qumram Evidence," *New Testament Studies* 43 (1997): 604–9.

19. Bruce, *1 and 2 Thessalonians,* 84.
20. Ibid.
21. 2 Corinthians 5:17.
22. Matthew 23:25–26.
23. 1 John 1:7.

Chapter 9: Solitary Refinement

1. Jacques Lacarrière, *Men Possessed by God* (Garden City, N.Y.: Doubleday, 1964), 57.
2. 1 Corinthians 7:32–35.
3. Susan T. Foh, *Women and the Word of God* (Phillipsburg, N.J.: Presbyterian and Reformed, 1979), 220.
4. Matthew 19:12.
5. This view is based on the belief that Paul was a member of the Sanhedrin, for which marriage would have been required. See W. J. Conybeare and J. S. Howson, *The Life and Epistles of St. Paul* (Grand Rapids: Eerdmans, 1983), 58, 64.
6. See 1 Corinthians 7:7–8.
7. Albert Y. Hsu, *Singles at the Crossroads* (Downers Grove, Ill.: InterVarsity, 1997), 178.
8. Anthony Storr, *Solitude: A Return to the Self* (New York: Ballantine, 1988), 55–88.
9. As quoted in William A. Heth, "Unmarried 'For the Sake of the Kingdom' (Matthew 19:12) in the Early Church," *Grace Theological Journal* 8 (spring 1987).
10. M. Thurian, *Marriage and Celibacy,* trans. N. Emerton (London: SCM, 1959), 81.
11. Mark 1:35 NIV.
12. Matthew 14:13 NIV.
13. Dietrich Bonhoeffer, *Life Together* (New York: Harper & Row, 1954), 77.
14. Ibid.

15. St. Francis de Sales, *Introduction to the Devout Life* (London: Burns, Oates, and Washbourne, 1934), 8–10.

Chapter 10: A Psalter for Psingles

1. Ephesians 4:25.

Chapter 11: Finishing Well

1. Arthur Bennett, ed., *The Valley of Vision: A Collection of Puritan Prayers and Devotions* (Edinburgh: Banner of Truth Trust, 1975).